HERBERT W. ARMSTRONG
and his
WORLDWIDE
CHURCH OF GOD

HERBERT W. ARMSTRONG
and his
WORLDWIDE CHURCH OF GOD

A Critical Examination

Roger F. Campbell

CHRISTIAN LITERATURE CRUSADE
Fort Washington, Pennsylvania 19034

CHRISTIAN LITERATURE CRUSADE
Fort Washington, Pennsylvania 19034

CANADA
1440 Mackay Street, Montreal, Quebec

GREAT BRITAIN
The Dean, Alresford, Hampshire

AUSTRALIA
P.O. Box 91, Pennant Hills, N.S.W. 2120

SBN 87508-061-8

This book is affectionately dedicated
to my wife, Pauline,
who has witnessed the flood of inquiry
about this subject,
and has urged me to prepare this book
to aid those in search of the truth.

CONTENTS

INTRODUCTION   9

1   HERBERT W. ARMSTRONG— A SUCCESSFUL
    MAN   11

~2 HERBERT W. ARMSTRONG'S TEACHING ON
    HEAVEN   17

~3 DOES HERBERT W. ARMSTRONG HEAD THE
    ONLY TRUE CHURCH ON EARTH TODAY?   23

4   HERBERT W. ARMSTRONG'S STRANGE TEACH-
    ING ON THE NEW BIRTH   31

5   HERBERT W. ARMSTRONG'S DOCTRINE OF
    SALVATION   39

6   HERBERT W. ARMSTRONG'S BIGGEST BIBLI-
    CAL BLUNDER   47

7   HERBERT W. ARMSTRONG AND THE TRINITY

                                              67
8   WILL HERBERT W. ARMSTRONG BECOME
    GOD?   75
9   HERBERT W. ARMSTRONG: CRUSADER
    AGAINST PAGANISM IN CHRISTMAS AND EAS-
    TER   85 ⌐

10 HERBERT W. ARMSTRONG'S SURPRISING
    STAND ON ALCOHOL AND WORLDLINESS! 91
11 YOUR QUESTIONS ANSWERED   97
12 WE ESCAPED FROM ARMSTRONGISM   105
    INDEX OF BIBLE QUOTATIONS   111
    INDEX OF QUOTATIONS FROM ARMSTRONG
    MATERIAL   117

INTRODUCTION

Since the publication of my article "Herbert W. Armstrong: Mr. Confusion," I have had numerous requests for more information about Mr. Armstrong and the teachings of The Worldwide Church of God, sometimes also called The Radio Church of God.

These requests have come in the form of hundreds of letters, many phone calls, and a number of personal visits, from people who have felt the effect of Armstrongism in their personal lives. It has been my privilege to assist some who had become confused by these strange doctrines.

Each chapter in this book deals with some specific area where Herbert Armstrong has departed from correct Bible interpretation. Along with the exposition of error, I have shared the approach that I have found to be the most helpful in leading people from Armstrongism to the Truth.

Some of the things revealed about Mr. Armstrong and his theology will be surprising. Some readers may even rebel at some of the facts presented, and may doubt their accuracy. In that event, it will be a simple task to check the references to Armstrong's material. To the best of my ability these references are carefully quoted, in their context, to present a true picture of Herbert W. Armstrong and his Worldwide Church of God. Anyone who reads Mr. Armstrong need not be told that all the capitals and italics are his.

It is my prayer that the positive presentation of sound doctrine, in this book, will not only refute Armstrongism, but will also serve to enrich the reader's faith.

ROGER F. CAMPBELL

Waterford, Michigan

Chapter 1

HERBERT W. ARMSTRONG— A SUCCESSFUL MAN

Herbert W. Armstrong is an unusually successful man. He is successful as a radio preacher. His letter to subscribers of *The Plain Truth* recently announced that he purchases more radio time than any other broadcaster in the world. He boasts that he is using more than fifty million watts of power weekly on nearly 400 stations worldwide. This broadcasting is carried on mainly by his son, Garner Ted Armstrong, at the present time. The broadcast was begun, however, and brought to success by Herbert W. Armstrong himself.

He is successful as a publisher. His magazine, *The Plain Truth,* claims a monthly circulation of over two million copies. His newer magazine, *Tomorrow's World,* is reported to have reached a circulation of nearly a half million.

He is successful as a religious promoter and leader. He claims to have 125,000 co-workers, a number of which meet regularly in meetings conducted by his ministers.

He has established three colleges. They are located at Pasadena, California; Big Sandy, Texas; and at Bricket Wood, England. They serve approximately 1400 students.

Perhaps Armstrong's words best sum up his evaluation of his work. He writes: "Today it is a truly great worldwide operation serving some 150 million people on all continents!"

His more recent letters tell of his new emphasis in the Far East. Appointments with leaders of a number of countries are mentioned, and Mr. Armstrong's pleasure is apparent in his reporting that he has a son of a member of the Japanese Diet (congress) attending Ambassador College.

Network television seems to be the new frontier for the Armstrongs. In a letter to co-workers, dated January 29, 1971, a proposed new project was announced in the following words:

> Whenever my son, Garner Ted, or I happen to see some of our co-workers personally, always the question is "WHEN am I going to be able to see the TELEVISION program in MY area?" Important meetings were held in Washington, D.C. last week with top officials of three of the great national television networks. Now talks are definitely on the way toward putting the program on the network.*
>
> . . . I can say now that the very top officials do LIKE the program. They have been much impressed with the highly professional quality—the photography, the intense interest of the subject matter; they simply can't understand how we could produce a program ourselves of such network quality. I can tell you, too, that television executives regard Garner Ted Armstrong as one of the most outstanding television personalities in the country.

What kind of man is this, who has brought his religious organization from a handful of followers to its present size?

First, he is evidently a man of great energy and ambition. His autobiography states that he at one time took a job that had been held by three men, all of whom were men of ability. Certainly any man who can successfully do the work of three able men is a man with great drive

---

*The June 1973 listing shows 56 TV stations in the U.S. and Canada carrying "The World Tomorrow" program, some of them daily.

and discipline. Who could deny that the work that Armstrong has headed in broadcasting and publishing has required long hours and hard work?

Besides that, Mr. Armstrong must be a man of exceptional self-confidence. On page 35 of the early booklet *The Autobiography of Herbert W. Armstrong,* he tells of an experience in seeking a position with an advertising manager. The manager informed him that he did not need any help, to which Mr. Armstrong says he replied:

> "Well then, do you mean to tell me that an organization of national scope and influence cannot—or is not interested in finding a way to create an opening for an ambitious, energetic young man like me? Do you realize that you probably don't get a chance once in several years to add a man of my caliber, my talents, and ambition and *will* to work to your staff? Why, you can't afford to pass up this opportunity; I'll *grow* with your organization—I'll develop rapidly into a very valuable man. *Of course you* can create an opening! As I said, I'll report for work the first Monday in next month."

Now if that isn't self-confidence, what is?

This same attitude is brought to almost unbelievable proportions in his comparison of experiences in his life to those in the life of Jesus and of the disciples.

He comments:

> Here then are the actual facts:
> First, Jesus Christ began His earthly ministry at about age 30. God took away my business, moved me from Chicago, started bringing me to repentance and conversion preparatory to inducting me into His ministry, *when I was 30!*
> Second, Jesus began the actual *teaching and training* of His original disciples for carrying HIS GOSPEL to the world in the year 27 A.D. *Precisely* 100 *time-cycles later,* in 1927 A.D., He began my intensive study and training for carrying HIS SAME GOSPEL to all nations of today's world.
> The actual ordination, or completing of the ordination and enduement of power for sending out the original disciples

into the ministry occurred after 3½ years of intensive instruction and experience. It was on the Day of Pentecost. And the year was 31 A.D.

Exactly 100 time-cycles later, after 3½ years of intensive study and training, Christ ordained me to preach this *same* Gospel of the Kingdom in all the world as a witness to all nations (Matt. 24:14). *This ordination took place at, or very near the Day of Pentecost, 1931* (*The Autobiography of Herbert W. Armstrong,* Volume I, pages 400 and 407).

To say that Herbert Armstrong believes himself to be a man of *divine destiny* might be the understatement of the century.

Probably the most important fact about Mr. Armstrong's success, however, is his great knowledge of successful writing and advertising. This has been his greatest tool in gathering his large following.

On pages 76 and 77 of his autobiography he describes some of his training in this field, and tells how it can be adapted to preaching and writing. He writes:

But in writing advertising, Mr. Boreman taught me always to *tell a story*—to make it *interesting*—and to tell it in *story form.* That is, first, put a question in the minds of readers they really *want* answered—or make a statement that is so unusual it either raises a question in the readers' minds, or challenges them to demand an explanation and want to read on to get it. It must arouse instant *interest*. It must create *suspense!* Like a mystery play, it must not tell the reader the answer at the beginning. It must develop, rapidly, lucidly, increasing the interest, toward the final solution or answer. It must HOLD the interest until the story is told.

The same principles apply to a spoken sermon or a Gospel Message advertisement. The headline: "WHY Does God *Allow Wars?*" followed immediately by a slightly smaller-type subhead saying: "If God is all merciful, he wouldn't *want* humans to suffer so terribly, would He? And if God is all-powerful, he *could* stop all this anguish. *Then why doesn't He?*" —this advertising headline, or the same words at the beginning of a sermon or a broadcast, makes people say either: "I've always wondered about that!" or, "I never thought of that —say, *that's interesting—I want to know the answer!!*" I have used this very beginning, in a full-page ad, in evangelistic sermons, and in the broadcast—and it has succeeded in getting the attention, arousing *interest,* and creating *suspense* to read on or listen through, of MILLIONS of people!"

Readers of publications of the Worldwide Church of God, and listeners to "The World Tomorrow" broadcast will recognize these advertising techniques admittedly used by Mr. Armstrong.

The full-color publications of this organization are eye-catching, and the articles all seem to carry the Armstrong flair for mystery and excitement, regardless of the topic being covered.

Because the Armstrongs seldom reveal their doctrinal position on their broadcast, "The World Tomorrow," many get on their bandwagon believing them to be fundamental Bible preachers declaring the historic Bible doctrines of other well-known radio ministries. It is not until the free literature arrives that the real story is told, and often that is presented so skillfully that the person is sold on these twisted teachings before he realizes it.

The chapters that follow will show that Armstrongism is far from being doctrinally sound or Biblically accurate, even though the movement has been successful.

It is time to tell the *plain truth* about Herbert W. Armstrong and his *world tomorrow.*

Chapter 2

HERBERT W. ARMSTRONG'S TEACHING ON HEAVEN

Watch the advertising expert in action in this heading on Garner Ted Armstrong's sermon on heaven.

Will You Get to HEAVEN?
Are your departed loved ones IN HEAVEN? Do Christians GO TO HEAVEN when they die? Are there really "MANSIONS IN THE SKY" waiting for you? Read the surprising, PLAIN TRUTH about these vital questions in your own Bible!

Do you see the exact pattern for capturing interest that Mr. Armstrong learned so well from his teacher? Certainly you do! Does it not excite your interest? These are *heart questions* of any person who has lost a loved one in death.

The first paragraph moves in this same gripping vein. He writes: " 'Gone to be with the Lord,' it is said of dead church-going people today. Is this literally true? Do people really GO TO HEAVEN when they die?"

Now if Garner Ted moved from this sensational beginning into the true Bible teaching on heaven, it would warm the heart and feed the soul, but I am sad to report that he does not do that.

With the hearts of his readers begging for bread, he gives them a stone!

Like the thief that robbed the poor traveler on the

Jericho road and left him half dead, he snatches away the hope of heaven. With a stroke of his pen, he moves all the saints of the ages from the delights of Glory to the darkness of the grave.

Listen to him:

> Think for a moment! How many sermons can you recall attempting to PROVE heaven is the destiny of Christians? Probably you can recall MANY where heaven was mentioned, was contrasted to a supposed ever-burning hell, or was *described.* Probably you have heard many *hundreds* of references to heaven as the final reward! But did you ever hear a sermon that PROVED it?
>
> No, You never did?
>
> Do you know why?
>
> Because it CAN'T BE PROVED! (*The Plain Truth,* Oct. 1961, page 16).

To all the people of God who have found strength and comfort in knowing that their loved ones are now in the presence of the Lord, Garner Ted Armstrong announces that "Going to heaven" is nothing more than a pagan doctrine that has been preached by deluded men.

Writing in *The Plain Truth* magazine, he declares:

> SHOCKING though it may sound—the Jesus Christ of your Bible *never* promised heaven as the reward of the saved! He promised something entirely different!
>
> Let's notice, FIRST OF ALL, the most-often quoted scriptures used by deluded men to preach the ancient, *pagan* doctrine of "going to heaven" (*The Plain Truth,* Oct. 1961, page 17).

Again he writes in the same article, "Notice—NO-WHERE DID JESUS SAY SAINTS GO TO HEAVEN!" (page 17).

Perhaps most confusing of all of Armstrong's statements about the state of man after death is found in Herbert W. Armstrong's article entitled "What is Man?", where he sets out to prove what happens to man at death. The following is a quote from that article:

> To continue with the question, "Who knoweth [whether] the spirit of man," that is the breath of man, "goeth upward, and the spirit of the beast," or the breath of beast, "goeth downward to the earth?"
>
> Well, does anyone know of it? It's a question. Who knows it? The answer is, "Nobody does" (*The Plain Truth*, March 1957, page 8).

Now *what are the answers to these perplexing questions raised by Armstrong's analysis of heaven?* Shall we cast aside our hope of immediately entering heaven upon death? Does Armstrongism have some new light that has been hidden from the great Bible students of the ages? Have Garner Ted and company spoken the last word on this vital subject?

Let us see what the Bible has to say to us about heaven. A simple fact about heaven to which, I believe, even the Armstrongs would agree, is that heaven is that focal point of the universe from which God operates, and in which is His throne. The Psalmist writes: "The Lord is in his holy temple, the Lord's throne is in heaven: his eyes behold, his eyelids try, the children of men" (Ps. 11:4).

Heaven is also the abode of the angels of God, Jesus said. "But of that day and that hour knoweth no man, no, not the angels which are in heaven, neither the Son, but the Father" (Mark 13:32).

The Old Testament records that two persons were taken immediately to heaven without experiencing death. These men, Enoch and Elijah, were "translated" that they should not see death and were taken directly to heaven. The writer of II Kings describes the translation of Elijah as follows:

And it came to pass, when the Lord would take up Elijah *into heaven* by a whirlwind, that Elijah went with Elisha from Gilgal. . . . And it came to pass, as they still went on, and talked, that, behold, there appeared a chariot of fire, and horses of fire, and parted them both asunder; and Elijah went up by a whirlwind *into heaven* (II Kings 2:1,11).

Further evidence that Elijah was taken to heaven is his appearance, along with Moses, on the mount of transfiguration, where both of these giants of the Old Testament discussed the coming death of Jesus with the Saviour.

Jesus surprised the scribes and the Pharisees by telling them that the inhabitants of heaven have great interest in the spiritual condition of men on earth. In Luke's record, the fifteenth chapter, Jesus is quoted as having said: "I say unto you, that likewise joy shall be in heaven over one sinner that repenteth, more than over ninety and nine just persons, which need no repentance" (Luke 15:7).

While Mr. Armstrong dissects this text and seeks to eliminate it as a promise of heaven, the fact remains that thousands of Christian people have claimed the promise that Jesus gave to his disciples: "In my Father's house are many mansions: if it were not so, I would have told you. I go to prepare a place for you" (John 14:2).

Paul, the apostle, reveals that every Christian is a citizen of heaven. He encourages the church at Philippi with the promise that "our conversation [Old English for "citizenship"] is in heaven" (Phil. 3:20). Would it not seem strange that a citizen of heaven would never have the privilege of visiting that country?

He confides with them that while he is thrilled with living, he is confident that death will be even greater, since death will simply be to "depart and to be with Christ: which is far better" (Phil. 1:21-23). That hardly sounds like the attitude of a man who expects death to be only a trip to the cemetery to await the resurrection.

He further assures the Corinthians that " . . . whilst we are at home in the body, we are absent from the Lord: (For we walk by faith, not by sight:) we are *confident,* I say, and willing rather to be absent from the body, and to be *present with the Lord"* (II Cor. 5:6–8).

To any of the Corinthians who might still doubt the reality of going to heaven, Paul explains the experience of being "caught up into paradise," where he speaks of hearing "unspeakable words which it is not lawful for a man to utter" (II Cor. 12:4).

Peter adds his voice to those of the other inspired apostles in anticipating the joys of heaven by speaking of "an inheritance incorruptible, and undefiled, and that fadeth not away, reserved in heaven for you" (I Pet. 1:4).

It is to the apostle John, however, that our Lord gives the privilege of previewing the scenes of Glory as they are recorded in the book of Revelation. There, in that panorama of the ages, he erases all doubt about heaven and who will be there.

Allowing us to get a glimpse of Glory, he speaks of the four and twenty elders before the throne. This is clearly a scene from heaven that takes place while the Great Tribulation is in progress on the earth. Of that scene he writes:

> And they sung a new song, saying, Thou art worthy to take the book, and to open the seals thereof: for thou wast slain, and hast redeemed us to God by thy blood out of every kindred, and tongue, and people, and nation: and hast made us unto our God kings and priests: and we shall reign on the earth (Rev. 5:9–10).

If there remains yet one skeptic, let him read Revelation 6:9–11. Here is a prophetic picture of those souls in heaven which have been slain in the misery and persecution of the Tribulation time. In heaven they cry out to the Lord to avenge their blood upon those that are still dwelling upon the earth.

> And when he had opened the fifth seal, I saw under the altar the souls of them that were slain for the word of God, and for the testimony which they held: and they cried with a loud voice, saying, How long, O Lord, holy and true, dost thou not judge and avenge our blood on them that dwell on the earth? And robes were given unto every one of them; and it was said unto them that they should rest yet for a little season, until their fellow-servants also and their brethren, that should be killed as they were, should be fulfilled (Rev. 6:9–11).

Do you see how *plain* the Lord has made this great *truth* that Christians *do* go to heaven immediately after death? What a wonderful hope it is!

I am pleased that we can reject Armstrong's statement, ". . . so Christians are not going to heaven after all" (*The Plain Truth,* Feb. 1958, page 20). For I have it on far better authority that Christians *are* going to heaven "after all." *After all* the problems of this life; *after all* the sickness and sorrow; yes, the Christian *is* going to heaven *"after all."*

Chapter 3

DOES HERBERT W. ARMSTRONG HEAD THE ONLY TRUE CHURCH ON EARTH TODAY?

It takes a lot of courage to announce to the world that you and your followers constitute the *only* true church on earth today.

Not only that, but it turns off a lot of radio listeners and literature readers.

Most people are slow to believe that one group has cornered all the truth in the Bible, to the exclusion of all other students of the Scriptures.

No one knows this better than Herbert W. Armstrong himself, and so he is very careful in his presentation of this fact.

It is really quite interesting to watch him, or his writers, work at presenting this part of their belief without really saying it.

This game of editorial "hide and seek" is aimed at pointing out all of the characteristics that the true church is to have, with an obvious elimination of all other groups, hoping that, by the process of elimination, the reader will choose The Worldwide Church of God as the one church that fits the description.

In his article "Why a Church?" published in the August 1962 issue of *The Plain Truth,* Garner Ted Armstrong wrote:

23

"*Where* is that true Church of which Jésus spoke—the Church he built—the Church He still RULES today?" It was prophesied to be a LITTLE flock, little-known by the world, suffering vicious attacks and persecution, but, true to Christ's prophecy, GROWING until it became a GREAT WITNESS TO ALL THE WORLD—*a witness the world could no longer* IGNORE!

That Church, the CHURCH OF GOD, GOD'S Church, the ONE and ONLY CHURCH JESUS BUILT, is on this earth today! Jesus said so.

Somewhere, somehow, there *is* on this earth a small but faithful group, living by the commandments of God (Rev. 12:17), following the WORD of God, not only preaching but PRACTICING the words of Christ—and proclaiming to all the world the GOOD NEWS of the coming KINGDOM OF GOD on this earth—the way the world WILL BE—TOMORROW! (page 43).

Notice that while Garner Ted does not come out with a strong statement that his father's work is the only true church on earth, he does end this paragraph on identification with an unmistakable reference to his radio broadcast, "The World Tomorrow."

An article titled "Here's Why the Word of God Is the Foundation of Knowledge" continues this search for the true church, stating:

Somewhere on earth today, the *one* true Church of God flourishes—it could never die (Matt. 16:18).

And so it now becomes *your responsibility* to find *God's* true Church. And to prove it.

How do you do it? The Bible gives clear-cut instructions. Which Church is literally called "The Church of God," is obeying *God's* Law, is a little flock, and is preparing the way for Jesus Christ's triumphant return by preaching and publishing the GOOD NEWS OF TOMORROW'S WORLD? The answer should be obvious. (*Tomorrow's World,* May–June 1970, page 14).

Yes, the answer certainly should be obvious to the reader, when the very title of the magazine he is reading is *Tomorrow's World.*

"How Would You Recognize the Church Jesus Founded?" That is the title of an article by Herman L. Hoeh, appearing in *The Plain Truth* of June 1968. The subtitle asks two more questions: "For what PURPOSE did Jesus found His Church? What WORK will it be doing today?"

In this article Mr. Hoeh zeroes in tactfully on the true church in the following words:

> His Church—the true Church of God—is commissioned to preach and to publish the Gospel to all the world IN THESE LAST DAYS. *Therefore God's Church* MUST EXIST TODAY! It is preaching the "Gospel of the Kingdom . . . in all the world for a *witness"* —not to convert everyone, but for a witness— "unto all nations, and then shall the end come" (Matt. 24:14).
>
> There is ONLY ONE WORK, that is preaching Jesus' Gospel of the Kingdom of God—the rule and the reign of God—to the nations. Then those who have their part in that Work and are converted MUST CONSTITUTE THE CHURCH OF GOD!
>
> You are challenged to prove which Work is preaching the same Gospel of the Kingdom—the rule—of God which Jesus preached!" (pages 42–43).

While the above is typical of the Armstrong approach to the "one true church" issue, there are times when Mr. Armstrong and his staff seem confident enough to come out with strong statements on their exclusiveness. They evidently feel that after sufficient preparation, there are times when their followers can digest such strong meat. For example, an article in *The Plain Truth* of February 1958 seems to throw all caution to the winds with the claims that Armstrong's Church of God is the only true church and that all others are satanic counterfeits. The words of the article are clear and unmistakable:

There is ONLY ONE WORK that is preaching the true gospel of the kingdom of God—the rule and the reign of God—to the nations. *This is that work.* Then those who have their part in this work and are converted MUST CONSTITUTE THE CHURCH OF GOD!

Every other work rejects the message of Jesus Christ or else rejects His rule through His laws. There is no exception.

Yes, this work is the work of the true Church of God. All others are satanic counterfeits! It is time we come out from among them and become separate (page 23).

Roderick C. Meredith nails it down equally as solid in his article, "The True Church—Where Is It?" (*The Plain Truth,* March 1963, pages 44–45).

He disposes of the thought that any other church might be used of God by stating:

The churches of this world have FAILED to grow in the *understanding* of the prophecies and of God's PLAN of salvation and His purpose in dealing with individuals and nations here on earth! *There is only* ONE *Church on earth* which has shown itself willing *to admit error, change* when necessary, and GROW in grace and in knowledge continuously and consistently!

Finally, there is only ONE SOURCE in all the earth—from Pasadena to Palestine, from Antarctica to the Bering Straits —which is really proclaiming the DEFINITE and SPECIFIC prophecies of God's Word to the nations of Israel and to the entire world as a final witness! This is the ONLY Church which is proclaiming the full MEANING of world events and the great PURPOSE and LAWS of human existence! This is GOD'S Church—and as God intended, it is named "The Church of God!"

Having disposed of all other denominations and religious groups as "satanic counterfeits," Mr. Armstrong might have been faced with a fairly serious problem had it not been for the resourceful research department of Ambassador College.

You see, before beginning his radio work Herbert Armstrong had been ordained to the ministry by *another* church, the Church of God with headquarters at Stanberry, Missouri.

True, he was ordained by the Oregon Conference —separately incorporated—but any honest reader might still be tempted to ask if this did not mean that Herbert had been ordained by a group of Satan's servants.

Fortunately for Mr. Armstrong, the Ambassador College researchers were able to identify that church as the dying or dead remnant of the "Sardis era" of God's true church (*The Autobiography of Herbert W. Armstrong,* Volume I, page 505). So, happily, Herbert was spared the embarrassment of a false ordination!

Now, seriously, let us face these inescapable questions: Is every church on earth of the devil if it is not part of the Armstrong organization? Is every Bible institute, college, and seminary except those founded by Armstrong producing graduates who will present a message that is a satanic counterfeit of the true gospel? Is every pastor, missionary, and evangelist that you have ever heard, except those associated with The Worldwide Church of God, a *servant of Satan?*

Honest people need to meet these questions squarely before they support or become a part of Armstrongism.

Let us go a step further.

Can it be true that every Sunday morning service ever conducted by faithful Christian people through the centuries since the beginning of the church has been in vain? *Certainly not!* Yet Herman Hoeh, senior editor of *Tomorrow's World,* has stated: "God has not convoked weekly religious meetings on Sunday morning!" ("A True History of the True Church," *The Plain Truth,* Jan. 1959, page 29).

To properly comprehend how justified Armstrong feels

in his exclusiveness, you must understand how important he thinks it was to the fulfillment of prophecy that he began his broadcast in 1934. Let him speak for himself:

> On the first Sunday in 1934, God's time had come. God opened a DOOR! Jesus Christ himself had foretold this event! Millions have read his prophecy.
>
> Yet on that first Sunday in 1934, probably NO one—certainly not I myself—recognized what a momentous event actually was taking place.
>
> What really occurred that Sunday morning precisely at 10 o'clock was a momentous event. It was the fulfilling of a definite corner-stone prophecy of Jesus. More than that, it was *the initial, start-off event of the fulfilling of some 90% of all the prophecies in the Bible!* And approximately *a third of the whole Bible* is prophecy! (*The Plain Truth*, Jan. 1959, page 3).

There you have it in Mr. Armstrong's own words. He believes that 90% of all the prophecies of the Bible, which he says make up nearly one third of all the Scriptures, hinged on the beginning of his radio broadcast in 1934. No wonder he has the courage to claim his organization is the *one true church!*

How different is all this from the clear teaching of the Apostle Paul that the true church is made up of all saved people wherever they may be! The Bible presents the true church as an organism, rather than an earthly organization.

To the Corinthians Paul wrote:

> For as the body is one, and hath many members, and all the members of that one body, being many, are one body; so also is Christ. For by one Spirit are we all baptized into one body, whether we be Jews or Gentiles, whether we be bond or free; and have been all made to drink into one Spirit (I Cor. 12:12–13).

It was to the saints (all those who had received Christ)

that Paul declared: "For we are members of his body, of his flesh, and of his bones. . . . This is a great mystery: but I speak concerning Christ and the church" (Eph. 5:30, 32).

If you have been born anew through faith in Christ, you are a member of the true church of our Lord and Saviour.

Chapter 4

HERBERT W. ARMSTRONG'S STRANGE TEACHING ON THE NEW BIRTH

It is said that when John Wesley was asked why he preached so often on the subject "Ye Must Be Born Again!" that he answered: "Because *you must be born again!*"

Wesley's definition of the new birth, however, would never have satisfied Herbert W. Armstrong, because one of the basic doctrines of Armstrongism is the teaching that you *cannot* be born again in this life.

Armstrong begins his booklet titled: *Just What Do You Mean—Born Again?* by ridiculing those who think they have experienced the new birth. He begins:

> LET'S be honest—don't some of these religious terms seem vague, meaningless, when you stop to think about it?
>
> Do you know that most people who think they have been "born again" actually have no more real conception of what it means than the young man who said he "gave his heart to the Lord" at a revival meeting. When asked if he had his chest cut open so he could reach in, take his heart out, and hand it to the Lord, he stammered confusedly that he guessed he didn't really know what it did mean, when he had been told that he "gave his heart to the Lord" (page 3).

It is tempting, after this slap at every true Christian, to just dismiss Armstrong's false teaching on the new birth by stating that since Mr. Armstrong clearly admits he has not yet been born again, he is not qualified to teach anything about the subject! Since this error, however, is so vital to an understanding of the rest of his theology, let us deal with it fairly and thoroughly in the light of the Bible.

Briefly, Herbert Armstrong teaches that the new birth is not the conversion experience, but is rather what takes place at the resurrection. He refers to conversion as being similar to conception, and says that the Christian is like an unborn babe in its mother's womb, finally to be born at the resurrection.

Perhaps this quote from his booklet *Why Were You Born?* gives the clearest picture of his teaching on this subject:

> God sent His Son Jesus Christ into the world as a human being, to pay for us, in our stead, the *penalty* we have incurred by the transgression of God's spiritual Law. So the second step in our salvation—our SPIRITUAL CREATION—being BORN of the Spirit—is to accept Christ Jesus as personal Saviour, being baptized for the remission of sins. Then God's PROMISE is that we shall receive HIS HOLY SPIRIT. And that is the entrance of the very LIFE of God—the impregnating "germ," so to speak, of eternal life—the begettal of the life of GOD. We then compare to an unborn babe in its mother's womb. And after the experiences of the Christian life, *if we overcome, grow in grace and knowledge,* and endure unto the end, then *at the time of the* RESURRECTION, this MORTAL SHALL BE instantaneously CHANGED INTO immortality—this flesh and blood body shall BECOME a SPIRIT body! Then, and not until then, shall we be FULLY BORN OF GOD (page 13).

Mr. Armstrong explains that the source of all this confusion about the new birth springs from a misleading translation of the Greek word *gennao*. Under the heading "Misleading Translation" he writes:

Since the original Greek, in which the New Testament was written, has *only the one word for both meanings*—and since the "scholars" of our comparatively recent years who translated the Bible into English did not, themselves, UNDERSTAND God's Plan—they often translated the Greek word "gennao" into the English word "BORN" where it actually *meant* "BEGOTTEN." (*Just What Do You Mean—Born Again?*, page 7).

As an example of a place where *gennao* is correctly translated as "begotten," Armstrong makes reference to I Corinthians 4:15:

". . . for in Christ Jesus I have *begotten* you through the gospel." There it is correctly translated, showing that Paul's converts at Corinth as his "spiritual children" had been *begotten* of God, *but not yet* BORN: (*Just What Do You Mean—Born Again?,* page 8).

But did Paul actually think of the Corinthian Christians as mere fetuses, babies yet to be born, as Armstrong contends? A look at I Corinthians 3:1-2 will reveal Paul's concept: "And I, brethren, could not speak unto you as unto spiritual, but as unto carnal, even as unto babes in Christ. I have fed you with milk, and not with meat: for hitherto ye were not able to bear it, neither now are ye able." So we see that Paul considered them to be sucklings who were already sufficiently past their birth that they should instead be chewing on solid food. These verses, of course, do not conflict with 4:15, but only with Armstrong's misapplication of it.

Armstrong also attempts to show how a number of texts would be changed by using the word "begotten" where it is now translated "born." By doing this he builds his case for showing that one is not really born again at conversion, but simply conceived as a child of God, with the new birth not taking place until the resurrection.

He even makes this apply to Jesus Christ! Read and wonder:

> Jesus was born once—as a human—of the virgin Mary. He was—at that time—born a HUMAN being, a descendant of David, who could die. He was *begotten* (not born —*begotten*) of God, in a manner such as no other human ever was begotten. So far as begettal for His *human* birth is concerned, Jesus was the ONLY human ever so begotten—God's *only* begotten Son.
>
> But Jesus also—in addition—was divinely begotten through God's Holy Spirit, *even from the moment of human birth, to be* BORN AGAIN—this time made the *divine* Son of God by the resurrection from the dead (Rom. 1:4).
>
> Thus, as VERY GOD, since His resurrection, He was the *first* so born of MANY BRETHREN! ". . . that He might be the firstborn among many brethren" (Rom. 8:29). This being the "firstBORN" cannot apply to His human birth at Bethlehem. (*Why Marriage! . . . Soon Obsolete?*, page 31).

In the same book he states: "It is correct to say, then, that Jesus was 'BORN AGAIN!' 'Firstborn,' not as a human, but as GOD 'by the resurrection!' " (page 31).

In all my study of the work of Herbert Armstrong in the last fifteen years, his claims here are some of the most surprising to me.

Mr. Armstrong is a careful man. He is a master at keeping himself out of a corner. Yet, here he makes statements that even a limited amount of thought and study will challenge.

What strange questions are raised by Mr. Armstrong's confused conclusions about Christ!

If Christ was conceived in Mary by the Holy Spirit and born naturally at Bethlehem, but not spiritually until the resurrection, was He then just a spiritual fetus all through His earthly life and ministry?

Was it a spiritually immature individual (though admittedly sinless) who healed the sick, raised the dead, and died for sinners?

If Jesus was "born again—by a resurrection into the very divine GOD FAMILY" (*Why Marriage! . . . Soon Obsolete?*, page 30), to what family did He belong prior to His resurrection? Did He belong only to the human family? If so, why was He so often called "the Son of God" during His life and ministry?

Consider also Mr. Armstrong's statement that there is only one word in the Greek New Testament to cover both meanings of conception and birth. That simply is not the case and shows a lack of homework on Herbert's part.

In addition to the word *gennao* the following Greek words are used:

> *Sullambano* is translated "conceive" in Luke 1:24, 31, 36; 2:21.
> *Tikto* is translated "delivered," "bring forth," "brought forth," or "born" in: Luke 1:31, 57; 2:7, 11; Matthew 1:21, 23, 25; 2:2; John 16:21; Revelation 12:2, 4, 5, 13.
> *Katabole spermatos* is translated "conceive seed" in Hebrews 11:11.

Now as to his comparison of conversion to conception instead of the new birth, see how absurd the verses listed below would be if the new birth did not take place at conversion:

> Being born again, not of corruptible seed, but of incorruptible, by the word of God which liveth and abideth forever. For all flesh is as grass, and all the glory of man as the flower of grass. The grass withereth, and the flower thereof falleth away: but the word of the Lord endureth for ever. And this is the word which by the gospel is preached unto you. Wherefore laying aside all malice, and all guile, and hypocrisies, and envies, and all evil speakings, as newborn babes, desire the sincere milk of the word, that ye may grow thereby (I Pet. 1:23—2:2).

That we henceforth be no more children, tossed to and fro, and carried about with every wind of doctrine, by the sleight of men, and cunning craftiness, whereby they lie in wait to deceive; but speaking the truth in love, may grow up into him in all things, which is the head, even Christ (Eph. 4:14–15).

The Christian life calls for birth, growth, and maturity, and these certainly are not possible if we remain only in the fetus stage throughout our lives.

Look at Mr. Armstrong's description of approximately how much of the Holy Spirit a Christian has in him. Speaking of one who has just been converted, he gives this description:

> He is now BEGOTTEN of God. The very LIFE and NATURE of God has entered into him impregnating him with immortal spirit-life, exactly as the physical sperm-cell from the human father enters into the ovum or physical egg-cell when a new HUMAN LIFE is first CONCEIVED, IMPREGNATED, OR BEGOTTEN. But, just as that tiny ovum, as small as a pinpoint, is merely begotten of its human father—NOT YET BORN—so the converted human is, at what we properly call conversion, merely BEGOTTEN of God the heavenly Father—NOT YET BORN.
>
> He is still material FLESH, even though God's Spirit has now entered into his MIND. He is still VISIBLE.
>
> And now he has about as much of God's Holy Spirit in him, by comparison, as the tiny human sperm-cell compares in SIZE to a baby being born. A human sperm-cell from which human life generates is about one-hundredth part as large as the egg-cell, which is about the size of a pinpoint. The sperm-cell is much too small to be seen by the human eye, without a microscope. (*Just What Do You Mean—Born Again?*, page 11).

Well, there you have it! Now you have Mr. Armstrong's conception of conversion . . . or should we say his version of spiritual conception?

At any rate, it is a sad description of the great work of God that takes place at the moment of salvation, and would seem to rob God of His glory by changing the mighty conversions of the Bible to mini-conversions of microscopic impact.

What a contrast to this is Paul's injunction to the Ephesians to be "filled with the Spirit" (Eph. 5:18)!

Let us get it clear now! According to the Bible, the new birth takes place at the moment of receiving Jesus Christ (John 1:12–13; John 3:1–16; I John 5:1).

In view of this plain teaching of the Scripture, let everyone who knows that he has been born of the Spirit see that he is daily growing in the grace and knowledge of our Lord and Saviour, Jesus Christ (II Pet. 3:18).

Chapter 5

HERBERT W. ARMSTRONG'S DOCTRINE OF SALVATION

Now we have reached the heart issue of this study. A lot can be endured in difference of Bible interpretation if a man is right in his teaching of God's plan of salvation. Men may differ on events of prophecy, systems of church government, or some of the so-called non-essentials of the faith, but in this one important area a man must be either right or wrong. There is no middle ground or room for debate. There is but one way of salvation!

Armstrong is wrong in his statement: ". . . the Bible reveals that NONE is yet 'saved'!" (*Why Were You Born?*, page 11).

While tens of thousands have given testimony to the saving power of God in their lives, Mr. Armstrong believes that not one person has yet been saved, and cannot be "saved" until the resurrection.

Armstrong's writers seem to enjoy poking fun at those who invite people to experience salvation now.

Writing in *The Plain Truth* in March 1957, Roderick C. Meredith scorned the work of present-day evangelists in the following words:

> Many people contend that there are many evangelists stomping up and down the land telling their audiences about the *reality* of Jesus Christ and *His shed blood* and calling upon them to "accept Christ and be saved."

"Come up and give your heart to the Lord tonight," they plead. "Won't you come? Come now while the Spirit is moving you. Come up and say, Tonight I accept Jesus Christ as my personal Saviour from sin."

Garner Ted Armstrong joins the ridicule refrain in his article "Please Don't Give Me 'That Old-Time Religion,' " published in the February 1968 issue of *The Plain Truth,* where he asks:

Just how *does* it sound, to an educated, fairly intelligent businessman, to hear frantic pleas of "Ohhhhh, WON'T you come—just now—and GIVE your heart to the Lord??" (Often pronounced "lard").

How DOES it sound to millions of frustrated youths, facing Vietnam, the bomb, and seemingly useless future, to be told with stentorian thunder, "CHRIST is the answer!!" (pronounced, oftentimes, "crast").

How many people are *really* given some meaningful goals to cling to when they hear, "REPENT sinner—right now (pronounced "rat naow")—and don't take a chance on goin' to hell" (sometimes pronounced "hail").

Why should anyone think it necessary to belittle sincere Christian people because their pronunciation of some words may not be as perfect as his own? Was it not D. L. Moody who wept publicly because he thought he did not speak the English language properly? Yet, only eternity will reveal the blessings to mankind, and the great number converted, through the work of this humble man.

The truth is, there are multiplied numbers of verses in the Bible that teach immediate salvation through faith in Jesus Christ, as the verses below demonstrate:

For the preaching of the cross is to them that perish foolishness; but unto us which *are saved,* it is the power of God (I Cor. 1:18).

Verily, verily, I say unto you, He that heareth my word,

and believeth on him that sent me, *hath everlasting life,* and shall not come into condemnation; but is passed from death unto life (John 5:24).

For by grace are ye [you have been] saved through faith; and that not of yourselves; it is the gift of God (Eph. 2:8).

Not by works of righteousness which we have done, but according to his mercy *he saved us,* by the washing of regeneration, and renewing of the Holy Ghost (Titus 3:5).

He that hath the Son hath life; and he that hath not the Son of God hath not life. These things have I written unto you that believe on the name of the Son of God; *that ye may know that ye have eternal life,* and that ye may believe on the name of the Son of God (I John 5:12–13).

While Herbert Armstrong denies it, he is also wrong in his mixture of grace and law for salvation.

In his booklet *What Do You Mean—Salvation?* he states that a few "persecutors" have accused him of teaching salvation by works, so he spends a good deal of time assuring his readers that he does not do so, and emphasizes that eternal life is God's *gift* through Christ. On page 21 of that same booklet he lists repentance, baptism, and faith in Christ as the means to experience "contact with God." Here again, he points out that it is only by the "gift" of the Holy Spirit that one can gain eternal life.

However, in his article "False Conversion," published in the October 1955 and the November 1966 issues of *The Plain Truth,* he explains that this *free gift* is conditional, and that you get it *only* if you "keep the commandments." So it turns out that the *free gift* is not free after all, and is given only if one is keeping the law.

Like the Seventh-Day Adventists, Armstrong insists that the keeping of Saturday (the Sabbath), is absolutely necessary for Christians today. He even goes so far as to state that salvation depends on the keeping of this law. On page 58 of his booklet *Which Day Is the Christian*

Sabbath? he calls the Sabbath command the only one of the Ten Commandments which is a *sign* identifying *who* are the real, true Christians today! He calls the Sabbath command "the one on which YOUR VERY SALVATION and ETERNITY DEPENDS!"

In addition to the keeping of the Sabbath, he teaches that there are seven festivals of the Old Testament that Christians today are to celebrate. That is why the followers of Herbert Armstrong still commemorate the feasts of Israel that in reality find their fulfillment in the death and resurrection of Christ. But what did Paul write: "Let no man therefore judge you in meat, or in drink, or in respect of an holyday, or of the new moon, or of the sabbath days; which are a shadow of things to come; but the body is of Christ" (Col. 2:16–17).

For a thorough and enlightening study concerning the purpose and significance of Israel's feast days I suggest the reading of *The Gospel in the Feasts of Israel,* by Victor Buksbazen.* Mr. Buksbazen describes Israel's experience in keeping the feast days that had been commanded in the Old Testament and explains how they all find their fulfillment in the person and work of Christ. Also included in the book are two chapters dealing with the Sabbath question and showing the Biblical and historic difference between the Sabbath and the Lord's Day.

In his epistle to the Galatians, Paul reminds his readers that neither the beginning nor the continuation of their salvation is dependent upon the keeping of the law. Notice how plainly he instructed the Galatians when he wrote to them to deal with this very problem:

> O foolish Galatians, who hath bewitched you, that ye should not obey the truth, before whose eyes Jesus Christ hath been

*The Spearhead Press, 475 White Horse Pike, West Collingswood, N.J. 08107 evidently set forth, crucified among you? This only would I learn of you, Received ye the Spirit by the works of the law, or by the hearing of faith? Are ye so foolish? having begun in the Spirit, are ye now made perfect by the flesh? (Gal. 3:1–3).

Christians are given a higher standard of holiness than the law, and this is made possible by the enabling of the indwelling Holy Spirit (Romans 8:1–4).

Not only is Herbert Armstrong wrong about the means and the way of salvation, he is also confused about its urgency.

One heading in his booklet *Predestination* is: "All Unsaved Not Finally Lost." Under this heading he labels as one of the greatest errors of this time the assumption that there are only two classes—the *saved* and the *lost.* Like the Jehovah's Witnesses, he then endeavors to prove that the great majority of those who are not saved now will be saved during the millennium. Compare the following two statements, the first from Armstrong's booklet and the second from *"Let God Be True"* (Jehovah's Witnesses).

(1) And *then* what shall happen during the thousand year reign from then on? . . . Here are the earth's nations—earth's mortals—*all* nations! And now begins a process of SEPARATION. It is according to the decisions they make, and the actions they take. Those who turn to a life of RIGHTEOUSNESS are set on the RIGHT hand. They are converted—given IMMORTALITY (*Predestination,* page 11).

(2) During Christ's millennial reign they will return from the realms of the enemy and will ultimately, if obedient, see the promise fulfilled. . . . At the end of Christ's reign, after successfully passing the final judgment test, these will attain to their justification to the right to life from Jehovah God (*"Let God Be True,"* page 282, Jehovah's Witnesses).

In his pamphlet *Is This the Only Day of Salvation?* Dr. C. Paul Meredith, one of Armstrong's writers, has written: "This is the long-awaited millennium. This is THE TIME GOD HAS SET TO REALLY START TO SAVE PEOPLE." Under the heading "When Is Vast Majority Saved?" he describes the Great White Throne Judgment, after which he announces: "SALVATION will be open to all then resurrected, just as in the *thousand-year* reign of Christ on earth, only now there will be *many more* to accept it after the millennium." He concludes the article with these words: "—then, AND ONLY THEN, it is that GOD REALLY starts to save the *vast majority* of mankind and give eternal life to those who are willing to come under His loving rule and aid HIM in administering wisely the great power He will share with them!"

Dr. C. P. Meredith, a contributing editor, wrote in the March 1957 issue of *The Plain Truth:* "God is not trying to save many now." This is as far from the gospel as a man can get!

In truth, the Bible finds both Herbert Armstrong and the Jehovah's Witnesses without basis for their offer of an opportunity for salvation after this life has ended. One basic scripture is Hebrews 9:27: "And as it is appointed unto men once to die, but after this the judgment. . . ."

While in his booklet *Lazarus and the Rich Man* Mr. Armstrong concludes that the rich man of Luke 16:19–31 did *not* find himself awake in hell immediately after the moment of death, the fact still remains that Jesus said: ". . . the rich man also died, and was buried; and in hell he lift up his eyes, being in torments" (Luke 16:22–23).

In his lifetime here on earth he had passed up all opportunity for salvation and immediately after death he found it was too late.

Try to reconcile the teaching that men will have time

for salvation after death, with the Great Commission (Matt. 28:18–20); or with Peter's explanation that Christ's second coming has not yet taken place because God is not willing that any should perish (II Pet. 3:4–9), and you have an impossible task.

The plain truth is that there is no other opportunity for salvation after this life is past. ". . . now is the accepted time; behold, now is the day of salvation" (II Cor. 6:2).

In summary then, it is Mr. Armstrong's lack of understanding of the experience of salvation, his mixture of law and grace, and his complete confusion about the urgency of becoming a Christian during our lifetime, that makes his teaching on salvation a deadly mixture of truth and error.

Chapter 6

HERBERT W. ARMSTRONG'S BIGGEST BIBLICAL BLUNDER

Someone has said, "Show me a man who is right about Israel and I will show you a man who is right about the rest of the Bible." That statement may not always be correct to the letter, but one thing is always sure: "Show me a man who is *wrong about Israel,* and I'll show you a man who is *wrong* about God's prophetic plan."

Herbert Armstrong is *wrong about Israel,* and this has become a source of error to him in many other areas.

Perhaps the most exciting of Armstrong's publications is his book *The United States and the British Commonwealth in Prophecy.* Here he discloses what he calls ". . . the vital KEY necessary to unlock closed doors of Biblical prophecy . . . ."

This 226 page book, copyrighted in 1967, contains maps and many full-color pictures and is written in most convincing language. It must be considered one of Armstrong's most important books. His own evaluation of the book is given on one of the opening pages where he announces that he thinks events during the next five years may prove it to be the *most significant book of the century.*

The autobiography of Mr. Armstrong reveals that as early as 1927–1930 he believed that he had located the lost ten tribes of Israel, and he reports that he submitted a manuscript of 300 typed pages on this subject to an editor and leader of the church he was then attending.

So convinced is Armstrong of his accuracy in identifying the lost ten tribes of Israel and other ancient peoples, as they appear today, that he claims this is the *key* to the understanding of prophecy.

Introducing his book he boasts:

> And why have these prophecies not been understood or believed?
>
> Because the vital KEY that unlocks prophecy to our understanding had been lost. That KEY is the IDENTITY of the UNITED STATES and the BRITISH PEOPLES in Biblical prophecy.
>
> That KEY has been found!
>
> We present it to those whose unprejudiced eyes are willing to see, in this book.
>
> The events prophesied to strike the American and British peoples in the next four to seven years are SURE!" (*The United States and the British Commonwealth in Prophecy,* Introduction, page xii).

But Mr. Richard Marson of Seattle, Washington, once an ardent follower of Armstrong, is not certain that these events *are sure* anymore.

Mr. Marson was captivated by Armstrongism for over ten years, and was especially influenced to accept these teachings through his study of *The United States and the British Commonwealth in Prophecy,* when it appeared in one of its earlier editions.

In the preface to his new book, *The Marson Report,** he describes Herbert Armstrong and his teaching on the United States and the British Commonwealth as follows:

> With newspaper in one hand and Holy writ in the other,

---

*The Ashley-Calvin Press, 8748 - 18th St., N.W., Seattle, Wa. 98107

Herbert W. Armstrong has been preaching the "soon coming—later than we think—downfall of the United States and British Empire" for nearly forty years.

Throughout Mr. Armstrong's long career the British and Americans have stood, it seems, on the bare "last gasp, bug eyed, choking" edge of final and chaotic oblivion. Final destruction was first slated for 1938; then 1969–1972; and now, 1979 or 1980.

Possessing "definite knowledge" and "vital keys," this man and his son, Garner Ted Armstrong, utter foreboding omens of certain calamity and doom while expressing unmistakable confidence that their own personal brand of interpretation must be right.

In the mind's eye, Mr. Armstrong sees most English speaking peoples as none other than the ancient Biblical house of Israel. To him, Germany must be the historic Assyrian Empire, and Italians descendants of the great Babylonian nation.

Mr. Marson further warns his readers not to fall for the convincing arguments put forth in this book. He pleads: "Do not make the mistake I made ten years ago when I accepted this theory without proving it. I accepted it and felt it was correct. But, I did not prove it" (*The Marson Report,* page 23).

The United States and the British Commonwealth in Prophecy is Herbert Armstrong's imaginative account of the history of the lost ten tribes of Israel and their identification today as the United States, the British Commonwealth nations,. and the nations of northwestern Europe.

In his own words:

The peoples of the United States, the British Commonwealth nations, and the nations of northwestern Europe are, in fact, the peoples of the TEN TRIBES of the HOUSE OF ISRAEL. The JEWISH people are the house of JUDAH (*The United States and the British Commonwealth in Prophecy,* page 164).

Summarizing Armstrong's teaching on the lost ten tribes of Israel, the reader finds that his doctrine divides into at least seven points:

1. That God's promises to Abraham to make his descendants as the dust of the earth and as the stars of heaven has never been fulfilled and will never be fulfilled in the people we now call the Jews.

2. That the ten tribes of Israel taken captive by Assyria have never returned to Palestine and have become the lost ten tribes, and that the terms "house of Israel," or "all Israel," when the meaning is national, or the terms "Jacob," or "Rachel," or "Ephraim," or "house of Joseph," or "Samaria," often used in the Bible in prophecy, relate to the ten-tribed birthright people, not to the Jews (*The United States and the British Commonwealth in Prophecy*, page 86).

3. That the peoples of the United States, the British Commonwealth nations, and the nations of northwestern Europe are, in fact, the ten tribes of the House of Israel.

4. That Great Britain is the tribe of Ephraim and that the United States is the tribe of Manasseh. These two nations are the birthright tribes, holding the birthright jointly, and that is the reason for the great riches and power of these two nations at their zenith.

5. That the throne of David was transplanted to Ireland by Jeremiah in the year 569 B.C., and that it was moved from there first to Scotland, and then to England, and that the Queen of England sits today upon David's throne.

6. That the stone under the queen's coronation chair is "Jacob's pillar-stone," which he took with him when he departed from Bethel, that was later brought to Ireland by Jeremiah when he came to transplant the throne of David.

7. That Bible prophecy relating to Israel refers, in reality, to the United States, Great Britain, and the nations

of northwestern Europe.

Now let us see what the Bible has to say about these doctrines that Mr. Armstrong teaches.

1. Certainly God did promise Abraham that He would make his seed as the dust of the earth and as the stars of the heaven. Remembering that the most reliable commentary on the Bible is the Bible itself, notice that both Moses and Solomon declared that those promises had already been fulfilled. Moses reminds the people of Israel of God's promise that they would be as the stars of the heaven for multitude and says that they had attained God's definition of that promise even then: "The Lord your God hath multiplied you, and behold ye are this day as the stars of heaven for multitude" (Deut. 1:10). Solomon was overwhelmed with the weight of responsibility given to him when he became the king in David's stead, and his prayer in the night for wisdom reveals that he considered his people even then to be "like the dust of the earth in multitude." He prayed: "Now, O Lord God, let thy promise unto David my father be established; for thou hast made me king over a people like the dust of the earth in multitude" (II Chron. 1:9). It is evident then that it would be dangerous to build doctrines demanding greater fulfillment than the Bible demands. Without doubt, this part of Armstrong's foundation for his Anglo-Israelism crumbles under careful investigation.

2. There is no question about the fact that the ten tribes of Israel were taken captive by Assyria. It is also true that the tribe of Judah was taken captive by Babylon. What is sometimes missed, however, is the fact that the Assyrian and Babylonian Empires covered essentially the same area. So it was that, when the later captivity took place, the inhabitants of Jerusalem and surrounding areas

were taken to the same general area that the other tribes had been taken to before them, when the area was ruled by Assyria, and at the time of the restoration the whole area was ruled by Persia. That is why there is evidence that representatives of all the tribes returned in the restoration.

Herbert Armstrong works hard to prove that the ten tribes are still lost, and are only found when identified as the people of Britain, America, and northwestern Europe. Under the section headed "Israel, Not Judah, Lost," he quoted Deuteronomy 32:26 as a proof verse to show that the remembrance of Israel was to be lost. He argues:

> In Deuteronomy 32:26, God had warned them through Moses: "I said, I would scatter them into corners, I would MAKE THE REMEMBRANCE OF THEM TO CEASE FROM AMONG MEN." That warning *cannot* be applied to the *Jew!!* The remembrance of them could not cease unless their identity and name were lost. This applies to the LOST tribes, not to the Jews (*The United States and the British Commonwealth in Prophecy,* page 88).

Sounds like a convincing argument, doesn't it? It is, unless you read Deuteronomy 32:27! But, of course, the average reader doesn't take the time to check out these references and so is captured by Armstrong's logic.

However, Richard Marson did finally read Deuteronomy 32:27, and so when he put his pen to work to help people see the errors of Armstrongism he exposed part of Mr. Armstrong's book with these words:

> After Herbert Armstrong states some facts concerning the ten tribes' captivity, he begins to wax eloquent in his assertion that these people became lost from view.
>
> Mr. Armstrong may have lost them but history does not lose sight of them for many centuries! Mr. Armstrong wishes

they would get lost, somewhere, by 585 B.C., so he could make his theory work, but they just do not disappear from view quite that easily. Herbert Armstrong needs to lose Northern Israel up in the British Isles by 585-530 B.C. to support his requirements that the throne must be built up in every generation.

He attempts to support his claim that the northern ten tribes quickly lost their identity, language, religion, land and name by quoting from Deuteronomy 32:26 . . . . He quotes as follows on page 88 of *The United States and the British Commonwealth in Prophecy:* "I said, I would scatter them into corners, I would make the remembrance of them to cease from among men." From this we gather that Israel would lose its identity. *But what about the very next verse——verse 27?* Let us put them together! "I said, I would scatter them into corners, I would make the remembrance of them to cease from among men: *were it not that I feared the wrath of the enemy, lest their adversaries should behave themselves strangely, and lest they should say, Our hand is high, and the Lord hath not done all this."* Deuteronomy 32:26–27 does NOT say God would cause Israel to lose its identity! (*The Marson Report*, pages 81–82).

Continuing this discussion of misinterpretations of scriptures, Mr. Marson shares this reflection on more than ten years of his life invested in following Armstrong:

> Were it not a great tragedy, some of Mr. Armstrong's misinterpretations would seem quite funny. I guess many have laughed at them. The seriousness of the situation is brought home to me, however, when I realize that he fooled me for ten years. Today he has about sixty thousand of his members fooled (*The Marson Report*, page 83).

Few would be fooled if they would simply lay aside Mr. Armstrong's full-color productions and concentrate on the message of the prophets concerning Israel. These godly men did not see Israel adopting a new land, or lands, as their own. Instead, they foresaw their people wandering, or being "sifted," through all nations, finally to return to their own land in the end time.

While each one of the prophets has a contribution to make concerning the future of his people, let us focus on the revelation that God gave to Amos about Israel.

> . . . I will not utterly destroy the house of Jacob, saith the Lord. For, lo, I will command, and I will *sift* the house of Israel *among all nations,* like as corn is sifted in a sieve, yet shall not the least grain fall upon the earth . . . . In that day will I raise up the tabernacle of David that is fallen, and close up the breaches thereof; and I will raise up his ruins, and I will build it *as in the days of old:* that they may possess the remnant of Edom, and of all the heathen, which are called by my name, saith the Lord that doeth this. . . . And I will plant them upon *their land,* and they shall no more be pulled up out of their land which I have given them, saith the Lord thy God (Amos 9:8–9, 11–12, 15).

See also: Ezekiel 37 (the entire chapter); Jeremiah 16:15, Hosea 3:4–5; Joel 3:1–7; Zechariah 7:14—8:8 and 9:9–12.

Now that we have established that Armstrong's basis for losing the ten tribes is false, let us notice how much evidence the Bible gives concerning the return of representatives of all the tribes of Israel to the land of Palestine. The books of Ezra and Nehemiah lay the foundation for our case: "And there went up some of the children of Israel, and of the priests, and the Levites, and the singers, and the porters, and the Nethinims, unto Jerusalem, in the seventh year of Artaxerxes the king" (Ezra 7:7). "So the priests, and the Levites, and the porters, and the singers, and some of the people, and the Nethinims, *and all Israel,* dwelt in their cities" (Neh. 7:73). "And the seed of Israel separated themselves from all strangers, and stood and confessed their sins, and the iniquities of their fathers" (Neh. 9:2).

Turning to the New Testament, we see that the apostle

Peter has no doubt as to the location of the *house of Israel* when, on the day of Pentecost, he states: "Therefore let all the house of Israel know assuredly, that God hath made that same Jesus, whom ye have crucified, both Lord and Christ" (Acts 2:36).

Anna, the prophetess, who was at the temple at the time of the dedication of the child Jesus, is called "the daughter of Phanuel, of the tribe of Aser" (Luke 2:36). The tribe of Aser is one of the tribes supposed lost by Mr. Armstrong.

Jesus called the disciple Nathanael an Israelite: "Jesus saw Nathanael coming to him, and saith of him, Behold an Israelite indeed, in whom is no guile!" (John 1:47).

Nicodemus, who came to Jesus by night, is described both as a "ruler of the Jews" and a "master in Israel" (John 3:1, 10).

Paul reveals that a number in the church at Corinth were Israelites and he compares their sacrifices in the service of Christ to his own as follows: "Are they Hebrews? so am I. Are they Israelites? so am I. Are they the seed of Abraham? so am I. Are they ministers of Christ? (I speak as a fool) I am more; in labours more abundant, in stripes above measure, in prisons more frequent, in deaths oft" (II Cor. 11:22–23).

The famous Pharisee, Gamaliel, addressed those men who plotted to do away with the apostles as "men of Israel" (Acts 5:35).

In his defence before Agrippa, Paul speaks with confidence about the twelve tribes of Israel. He declared:

> My manner of life from my youth, which was at the first among mine own nation at Jerusalem, know all the Jews; which knew me from the beginning, if they would testify, that after the most straitest sect of our religion I lived a Pharisee. And now I stand and am judged for the hope of the promise made of God unto our fathers: unto which pro-

mise *our twelve tribes,* instantly serving God day and night,
hope to come. For which hope's sake, king Agrippa, I am
accused of the Jews (Acts 26:4–7).

Jesus settled any question as to the location of the
house of Israel when He sent the disciples on a preaching
mission with the kingdom message. Clearly, Jesus is send-
ing these men to the immediate locality when He instructs
them saying: "Go not into the way of the Gentiles, and
into any city of the Samaritans enter ye not: but go rather
to the *lost sheep* of the *house of Israel.* And as ye go, preach,
saying, The kingdom of heaven is at hand" (Matt. 10:5–7).
The disciples obeyed that commission and returned to
the Saviour with a report of their ministry. Surely any
thinking person realizes that they did not travel to Great
Britain, or even the countries of Europe, during that brief
period.

Jesus said of His own ministry, that He was sent to
"the lost sheep of the house of Israel" (Matt. 15:24). Any
student of the New Testament knows that the ministry
of Jesus was carried on in the land of Palestine.

There is no question, then, that representatives of the
twelve tribes of Israel *did* return to the land of Palestine.
The proof of this is undeniable in both the Old and New
Testaments, and especially from the words of the Saviour
Himself. This combination of Bible facts should settle
the question for anyone willing to take the Scriptures
as his final authority.

3, 4. Once the true Bible teaching concerning Israel
is established, Armstrong's doctrines topple one after the
other like dominoes, and it would be foolish to waste
the reader's time proving that the people of Great Britain
and America are not Israelites.

Great Britain is not the tribe of Ephraim, and neither
is the United States Manasseh.

While Mr. Armstrong's vowel-dropping to make the sons of Isaac "SAAC'S SONS" and finally "SAXONS" may be intriguing, it simply does not stand up under careful study.

His hinting that the fact that there were thirteen original colonies may have some significant connection to the thirteenth tribe of Israel provides an interesting numbers game, but it has no basis in Bible interpretation.

The fact that the United States of America has great wealth *does not prove* that God's promise of prosperity for Israel is fulfilled in this nation.

Perhaps we should take a moment, however, to deal with Mr. Armstrong's inference that the wide distribution of the Bible among white, English-speaking people demonstrates the fact that we are really Israelites. On pages 14 and 15 of his book *The United States and the British Commonwealth in Prophecy* he has written:

> It is undeniable! Its history, from Genesis to Revelation, is primarily the history of one nation or people—the Israelites. Other nations are mentioned only insofar as they come into contact with Israel.
>
> All its prophecy, too, pertains primarily to this people of ISRAEL, and to other nations only insofar as they come into contact with Israel.
>
> The Bible tells of these Israelites and their God. It was inspired by the God of Abraham, Isaac and Jacob, committed to writing through Israelites exclusively, and was preserved until after the New Testament was written by these Israelites.
>
> In its sacred passages we read that all the promises and the covenants of God, all the sonship and the glory, belong solely to Israel (Romans 9:4).
>
> Yet we must face the astounding *fact* that our white, English-speaking peoples—NOT THE JEWS—have inherited the national and physical phases of those PROMISES!
>
> How could this have happened?
>
> The Bible is an Israelitish Book, preeminently of and for the Israelitish nationality, inspired by their God through their prophets!

Is it not, indeed, strange that we English-speaking peoples are the greatest believers in and exponents of this Book of the Hebrew people—that of all nations we are the chief worshippers of Israel's God and Israel's Messiah—in name and in form, if *not* in *truth* and in *deed?*"

But, would the wide distribution of the Scriptures (especially the New Testament) and acceptance of Christ as Messiah be an evidence that a nation was really populated by disguised Israelites?

Not at all!

Rather, it would be more likely to indicate that this was a Gentile nation. Israel has not experienced a wide acceptance of the Messiah, but instead a general rejection of Jesus Christ. Paul called it "blindness" and explained its existence and duration in his epistle to the Romans: "For I would not, brethren, that ye should be ignorant of this mystery, lest ye should be wise in your own conceits; that blindness in part is happened to Israel, until the fullness of the Gentiles be come in" (Rom. 11:25).

So, you see, the very suggestion that Armstrong uses in the opening pages of *The United States and the British Commonwealth in Prophecy* to condition his readers to accept his theory about Israel, is itself a refutation of the remainder of the book.

5. Was the throne of David transplanted to England, by way of Ireland and Scotland? Does the Queen of England sit today upon the throne of David?

The foundation for Armstrong's error in this area is his misunderstanding of the Davidic Covenant.

Since he evidently fails to consider some of the Bible verses that have to do with God's promise to David, he wrongly concludes that the covenant requires a literal earthly throne from the time of David to this day, and forever.

On page 67 of *The United States and the British Com-*

monwealth in Prophecy he quotes the promise to David from II Samuel 7:4-5 and 12-16:

> And it came to pass that night, that the Word of the Lord came unto Nathan, saying, Go and tell my servant David, Thus saith the Lord, Shalt thou build me an house for me to dwell in? . . . When thy days be fulfilled, and thou shalt sleep with thy fathers, I will set up thy seed after thee, which shall proceed out of thy bowels [Solomon], and I will establish the kingdom. He shall build an house for my name, *and I will establish the* THRONE *of his* KINGDOM FOREVER. I will be his father, and he shall be my son. If he commit iniquity, I will chasten him with the rod of men, and with the stripes of the children of men; but my mercy shall not depart away from him, *as* I took it from Saul, whom I put away before thee. *And thine house and thy* KINGDOM *shall be* ESTABLISHED FOREVER before thee: THY THRONE SHALL BE ESTABLISHED FOREVER.

On the following page he gives his interpretation:

> Here is the fact as little realized as any in the Bible! Almighty God made an absolutely binding—just how binding we shall see!—covenant with David, UNCONDITIONALLY guaranteeing that there should never be a single generation from that time forward when there would not be a descendant of David, in UNBROKEN DYNASTY, sitting on David's throne, ruling over the children of Israel! It was the promise of continuous unbroken DYNASTY—all generations *forever*—that was guaranteed.

But is the Armstrong interpretation correct? Must we search the world over to find a throne in existence at this present time that could be the throne of David? Did the Lord's promise to David guarantee that each generation from that day on would have a man in David's line sitting upon an earthly throne, regardless of the actions of David's descendants?

Once again, let us turn to the Bible for the answer.

Let the Psalmist speak: "The Lord hath sworn in truth unto David; he will not turn from it; Of the fruit of thy body will I set upon thy throne. *If* thy children will keep my covenant and my testimony that I shall teach them, their children shall also sit upon thy throne for evermore" (Ps. 132:11–12). David adds: "And he said unto me, Solomon thy son, he shall build my house and my courts; for I have chosen him to be my son, and I will be his father. Moreover I will establish his kingdom for ever, *if* he be constant to do my commandments and my judgments, as at this day" (I Chron. 28:6–7).

There is no question that God has established David's throne forever in Christ, the son of David. There is also no question about the fact that David understood that the literal establishment of that throne in his earthly descendants in the period between the giving of the covenant and the coming of the Messiah depended upon their obedience to the commandments of God. That was David's understanding of the covenant, as the above verses prove, and surely his interpretation is more dependable than that of Mr. Armstrong.

Add to this the prophecy of Hosea: "For the children of Israel shall abide many days *without* a king, and without a prince, and without a sacrifice, and without an image, and without an ephod, and without teraphim" (Hosea 3:4), and you have conclusive proof that there is no need, or purpose, in transplanting and transferring the throne to Ireland, Scotland, England, or any other place, until Christ Himself comes to fulfill the promise and to sit upon the throne of his father David *forever* (Luke 1:32–33).

6. Is the stone under the queen's coronation chair "Jacob's pillar-stone"?! Did Jacob carry it with him? And did Jeremiah carry it to the British Isles?

This, of course, has no Bible basis at all. Instead, the Bible teaches that Jacob *did not* take the "pillar-stone" with him, but left it for a memorial of God's faithfulness to him (Gen. 28:22; 35:14).

Jacob placed that stone as a memorial long before Israel had become a nation, or had ever gone to Egypt for the captivity. To imagine that Jacob returned and carried the stone later to Egypt, and that his descendants then brought it out of Egypt after four hundred years and carried it through the wilderness and to the promised land and finally on to England, not only seems improbable, but it does an injustice to the Scriptures.

Neither is there any evidence that Jeremiah ever went to the British Isles with the stone. In fact, the last glimpse we have of Jeremiah finds him in Egypt. His prophecies concerning the captivity of his people having come to pass, he now has been taken to Egypt by a small group of Jews who expect to escape from the king of Babylon. Jeremiah warns them that their effort is futile. His message is given in the form of the following object lesson:

> Then came the word of the Lord unto Jeremiah in Tah-panhes, saying, Take great stones in thine hand, and hide them in the clay in the brickkiln, which is at the entry of Pharaoh's house in Tahpanhes, in the sight of the men of Judah; and say unto them, Thus saith the Lord of hosts, the God of Israel; Behold, I will send and take Nebuchadrezzar the king of Babylon, my servant, and will set his throne upon these stones that I have hid; and he shall spread his royal pavilion over them. And when he cometh, he shall smite the land of Egypt, and deliver such as are for death to death; and such as are for captivity to captivity; and such as are for the sword to the sword (Jer. 43:8–11).

The interpretation is evident. Jeremiah prophesies that the king of Babylon will overcome Egypt. He further warns that death, captivity, or the sword await the remnant there.

Did then one of these befall Jeremiah along with his

countrymen? Many think so!

Herbert Armstrong, however, quotes Jeremiah 44:14 and 44:28 to show that Jeremiah escaped and ultimately made his way to the British Isles, carrying Jacob's "pillar-stone" and escorting the daughters of the king, there to plant the royal seed in that new land.

But let us look closely at those two verses.

> So that none of the remnant of Judah, which are gone into the land of Egypt to sojourn there, shall escape or remain, that they should return into the land of Judah, to the which they have a desire to return to dwell there; for none shall return but such as shall escape (Jer. 44:14).
>
> Yet a small number that escape the sword shall return out of the land of Egypt into the land of Judah, and all the remnant of Judah, that are gone into the land of Egypt to sojourn there, shall know whose words shall stand, mine, or their's (Jer. 44:28).

Notice that Jeremiah is not named as one who would escape, and even if he had been one of that "small number" his destination would have been Judah rather than the British Isles. Nor does it seem likely that Jeremiah would have left Judah to search for the ten tribes since he was a prophet to Judah.

Let is be made crystal clear that there is not one shred of Bible evidence that sends Jeremiah off to the British Isles. Of Armstrong's theory about Jeremiah's journey Richard Marson has commented:

> There has been much conjecture as to when and where Jeremiah died. Many authorities feel it probable that he died a short time later in Egypt. There is a Christian tradition that he was stoned to death by the Jews at Tahpanhes. An Alexandrian tradition reported that his bones had been brought to that city by Alexander the Great. On the other hand, there is a Jewish statement that, on the conquest of Egypt by Nebuchadnezzar, he, with Baruch, made his escape

to Babylon, and died there in peace. Poor old Jeremiah. Everyone wanted him. They wanted him up in Britain, too. In fact, Mr. Armstrong demands that he go there or else! But Scripture will not help Mr. Armstrong get him there! (*The Marson Report,* page 99).

As to the evidence of the substance of the stone itself, Mr. Marson states: "The stone in Westminster Abbey has been analyzed and shown to be a calcareous type of red sandstone of Scottish origin" (*The Marson Report,* page 128).

So, when the facts are all in, the "pillar-stone" becomes a "problem-stone" to the reliability of the theory Mr. Armstrong so enthusiastically supports.

Jacob left the stone at Bethel. Herbert Armstrong would have done well to do likewise.

7. Can the prophecies relating to Israel be applied to the United States and Great Britain, or European nations today? Nothing could be more misleading!

It is evidently because he has taken specific judgments pronounced against Israel, and wrongly applied them to the United States, that Garner Ted Armstrong has written:

> By the time slow-moving Russia is finally *ready* to strike, your Bible says America will have ceased to be a nation, her citizens removed-into a horrible captivity, and another totally *different* power will have risen—GERMANY! (*The Plain Truth,* July 1959, page 16).

The years since 1959 have proven that Russia is anything but "slow-moving" militarily, and Garner Ted Armstrong's prophecy has fallen because it is built upon a false foundation.

In what must be his most embarrassing book, *1975 in Prophecy,* Herbert Armstrong predicts:

But *this* time the Nazis plan to sidestep the causes of past defeats. Instead of exhausting their own strength by holding European nations as captives at the expense of vital Gestapo manpower, they plan to head and dominate a UNITED STATES OF EUROPE—and add the man-power of those nations to their own military divisions. And secondly, they plan to strike their *first blow,* NOT at France or Poland in Europe, but with hydrogen bombs by surprise attack on the centers of AMERICAN INDUSTRY! (pages 6–7).

While this coming Nazi-Fascist Colossus is developing underground, an alarming revolution is beginning to occur in the *weather.* Hurricanes, floods, sectional droughts are fast increasing.

While modern science and industry strive to prepare for us a push-button leisure-luxury-world by 1975, United States Assistant Weather Chief I. R. Tannahill warns us unofficially to really fear *"the big drought of* 1975." But the indications of prophecy are that this drought will be even *more* devastating than he foresees, and that it will strike *sooner* than 1975—probably between 1965 and 1972!

This will be the very *beginning,* as Jesus said, of the Great Tribulation!

Jeremiah's prophecy is more specific. It is the beginning of the NATIONAL trouble to come on America, the British nations, and the democracies of northwestern Europe! (pages 10–12).

Remember, now, that the above mentioned nations are those identified by Armstrong as Israel. That is the basis for his prediction.

He continues: "Here is exactly how catastrophic it will be: ONE THIRD OF OUR ENTIRE POPULATIONS will DIE in this famine and disease epidemic!" (page 12).

Armstrong says then that shortly after that the "Nazi-Fascist colossus" will strike its hydrogen-bomb blows and *another* third of our populations will be killed.

He then describes a *captivity* for Americans and Britons, whom he believes to be Israelites. Read his description of that coming captivity:

And that surviving third will be uprooted from their homes—transported like cattle *as slaves* to Europe, and probably some to South America (the Germans are fast gaining dominance and control in South America).

There they shall not only be forced under lashes of cruel taskmasters to do the work of slaves—but they will be forced to *give up* whatever belief they may have in real BIBLE Christianity! They will be literally *forced* to accept the idolatrous PAGAN beliefs and customs that masquerade as Christianity, or state police will arrest them, and they will be TORTURED inhumanly until they either give in, or die in martyrdom!

Yes, millions of lukewarm inactive professing Christians will suffer MARTYRDOM—and that *before* the anticipated push-button leisure year of 1975 dawns upon us! (page 20).

Here is ample proof of the erroneous conclusions to which this fascinating, but false, theory leads! Surely it is time, now, to accept the Bible evidence that the so-called lost tribes of Israel are *not* to be identified as the United States (a melting-pot of many different peoples), or even as Great Britain and certain northern European nations. Instead, the wise student of prophecy will turn his eyes to the work of God in the land of Palestine today, where the plan of God for His earthly people is unfolding in a dramatic way.

Chapter 7

HERBERT W. ARMSTRONG AND THE TRINITY

Like the Jehovah's Witnesses, Herbert Armstrong declares the doctrine of the Trinity to be a pagan teaching.

Compare the following quotes. The first is from the pen of Dr. C. Paul Meredith in *The Plain Truth,* February 1960. The second is from the book, *The Truth that Leads to Eternal Life,* published by the Watchtower Bible and Tract Society (Jehovah's Witnesses).

The Plain Truth:
Note now that the pagans termed the Holy Spirit a "Being" such as the Father and Son. They wrongly *made a Trinity.* SATAN WAS CONFUSING MANKIND.

Watchtower Publication:
What, then, do the facts show as to the "Trinity?" Neither the word nor the idea is in God's Word, the Bible. But you will be interested to know that . . . the pagans did believe in such a thing; in fact, they worshipped more than one trinity of gods.

Armstrong seems to be a bit unlike the "Witnesses" in his views concerning the Father and the Son, but appears to be identical to them in his teaching concerning the Holy Spirit. In their book *The Truth That Leads to Eternal Life,* the Jehovah's Witnesses define the Holy Spirit as "God's active force." In the above mentioned article by Dr. C. Paul Meredith in *The Plain Truth,* the Holy Spirit is called " . . . that divine force by which so much good is accomplished."

Even in regard to the Godhead, sarcasm is used to cut down those who disagree with Mr. Armstrong concerning the Father, Son, and Holy Spirit. See if you think the following comments border on blasphemy:

> Remember back to your high school days when there was a particular group you wanted to break into. Maybe it was the athletic clique, or perhaps the scholar's corner, or the popular cheerleader's circle. How painful it was when you were rejected because you didn't quite meet their standards. What an empty feeling to be in the "outgroup," to feel unwanted, rejected, not good enough.
>
> But do you know what's supposed to be the universe's most exclusive club—the clique from which all mankind is utterly excluded?
>
> It's the "trinity"! (*Tomorrow's World,* September–October 1970, page 30).

In this same article he declares that the Holy Spirit is not a divine Person, but "the power of God."

Perhaps it is Dr. C. Paul Meredith who spells out most concisely the Armstrong alternative to the teaching of the Trinity. He explains: "The true teaching of the Bible is that the Father and Son comprise the One Kingdom or Family of God. The Holy Spirit is the common nature, mind, and force of God" (*The Plain Truth,* Feb. 1960, page 26).

In his book *Why Marriage! . . . Soon Obsolete?,* Herbert Armstrong develops this doctrine more fully. On page 28 he illustrates:

> I am of the Armstrong *family.* We have had four children. I am "Armstrong." My wife was "Armstrong" also, from the moment she married me. Our son Garner Ted is "Arm

strong." We are two different *persons*—but we belong to the
ONE FAMILY. My son Richard David was a different *person,*
but he also was "Armstrong," and part of the Armstrong
family. The ONE Armstrong family.

So we were ONE family—but we were *six persons!*

Elohim is not two Gods, or three Gods, or many Gods
—Elohim is ONE God, but composed of *more than one divine
Person!*

And "Elohim" IS A DIVINE FAMILY!

Have you not thought of God as a PERSON—a single
PERSONAGE?

THE ONE God—*"Elohim"*—the ONE DIVINE FAMILY—*has
a Head.* He is the One we call the Father. His name is GOD.
Jesus called Him "Father." HE is the One most of us have
thought of as the PERSONAGE who is God. Jesus was His Son.
And Jesus, by a resurrection from the dead, is His divine Son
(Rom. 1:4), and Jesus also is GOD (John 1:1; Heb. 1:8).

Now, what does the Bible say?

First, let us establish the personality of the Holy Spirit
as it is described in the Bible.

When Jesus revealed the truth of the coming Comforter
(Holy Spirit) to the disciples, He said:

> Nevertheless I tell you the truth; It is expedient for you
> that I go away; for if I go not away, the Comforter will not
> come unto you; but if I depart, I will send *him* unto you.
> And when *he* is come, *he* will reprove the world of sin, and
> of righteousness, and of judgment. . . .Howbeit when *he,*
> the Spirit of truth, is come, *he* will guide you into all truth:
> for *he* shall not speak of *himself;* but whatsoever *he* shall hear;
> that shall *he* speak: and *he* will shew you things to come.
> *He* shall glorify me: for *he* shall receive of mine and shall
> shew it unto you (John 16:7–8, 13–14).

Notice the teaching of Jesus about this personal
member of the Trinity who can hear, speak, show, and
guide. Certainly this can never be said of a "force" as
Armstrong defines the Holy Spirit.

In addition, the book of Acts and the Epistles of Paul present the Holy Spirit as one who can be "grieved" (Eph. 4:30), "quenched" (I Thess. 5:19), and even "lied to" (Acts 5:3). Can you imagine a "force" being grieved?

Armstrong likens the Holy Spirit to electricity. Can you picture yourself lying to an electrical outlet? Of course not! Yet, Ananias was slain for lying to the Holy Ghost.

There is simply no doubt about the fact that the Bible describes the Holy Spirit as One who has intellect, emotion, and will, and those three factors make the difference between a personality and a force.

Here is proof:

The Holy Spirit has intellect. "The Spirit searcheth all things, yea, the deep things of God. For what man knoweth the things of a man, save the spirit of man which is in him? even so the things of God knoweth no man, but the Spirit of God" (I Cor. 2:10–11).

The Holy Spirit has emotion. "And grieve not the holy Spirit of God, whereby ye are sealed unto the day of redemption" (Eph. 4:30).

The Holy Spirit has a will. "But all these worketh that one and the selfsame Spirit, dividing to every man severally as he will' (I Cor. 12:11).

Accept these Bible truths and they will aid you in an understanding of the third Person of the Trinity.

Finally, we must face the question of whether or not the Bible teaches the relationship of the Father, Son, and Holy Spirit to be that of the historic definition of the Godhead.

Thousands of church covenants, or statements of faith, contain the words: "We believe in one God, eternally existing in three persons: The Father, the Son, and the Holy Ghost, and these three are one God." Are they correct?

Not according to Armstrong's writers contributing to

the September–October 1970 issue of *Tomorrow's World*. On page 31, writer L. Neff declares: " . . . the Bible *nowhere* even alludes to God being a trinity." On the same page B. McDowell adds: " . . . all scholars admit that there is *no reference* to the trinity in the Bible, but it is only, as they say, *'implied.'* "

How easy it is to marshal "all scholars" to your defense! Yet any student of the Bible knows that reference books abound on the subject of the Trinity. Does Mr. Armstrong wish to qualify these statements? Perhaps he should suggest that his writers may mean that all scholars at the Ambassador College admit that there is no reference to the Trinity in the Bible.

If Mr. Neff means that the actual word "Trinity" is not found in the Bible, he is correct. But surely "all scholars" should know that it is a "word of convenience" —like "theology," "millennium," and many others—long ago developed by Bible students to express Biblical truths in shortened forms. Though the word itself is not used, the Bible has a great deal to say about the Trinity in both the Old and New Testaments.

Consider first the evidence in the Old Testament. There, the Hebrew language assists us in an understanding of the Trinity.

The very first verse in the Bible contains the plural form of the word that is translated "God." From that point on the name of God will appear again and again, through the Old Testament, in the plural form *"Elohim."*

Plurality is also indicated in such statements as: "And God said, Let *us* make man in *our* image, after *our* likeness . . ." (Gen. 1:26). "And the Lord God said, Behold, the man is become as one of *us* . . ." (Gen. 3:22). "Go to, let *us* go down, and there confound their language, that they may not understand one another's speech" (Gen. 11:7).

Now, at this point, it is important to understand the meaning of the Hebrew word *echad* that is translated "one" in Deuteronomy 6:4: "Hear, O Israel: The Lord our God is one [*echad*] Lord."

The word *echad* is used to show "compound unity," as in the case of Numbers 13:23. There the spies are said to have brought back "one" cluster of grapes. It was one cluster, but made up of a number of grapes. It was a compound unity.

In short, then, the Hebrew words used for God and to describe God call for a plurality in unity.

But who are the Persons of this plurality?

The Old Testament reveals that one Person is the Father.

> A son honoureth his father, and a servant his master: if then I be a *father,* where is mine honour? and if I be a master, where is my fear? saith the Lord of hosts unto you, O priests, that despise my name. And ye say, Wherein have we despised thy name? (Mal. 1:6).
>
> Doubtless thou art our *father,* though Abraham be ignorant of us, and Israel acknowledge us not: thou, O Lord, art our *father,* our redeemer; thy name is from everlasting (Isa. 63:16).

The Bible further reveals that one Person is the Son.

> Who hath ascended up into heaven, or descended? who hath gathered the wind in his fists? who hath bound the waters in a garment? who hath established all the ends of the earth? what is his name, and what is his *son's* name, if thou canst tell? (Prov. 30:4).
>
> I will declare the decree: The Lord hath said unto me, Thou art my *Son;* this day have I begotten thee (Ps. 2:7). (See also Hebrews 1:5 in connection with this verse.)
>
> Kiss the *Son,* lest he be angry, and ye perish from the way, when his wrath is kindled but a little. Blessed are all they that put their trust in him (Ps. 2:12).

Finally, the third Person is the Holy Spirit.

> And the earth was without form, and void; and darkness was upon the face of the deep. And the Spirit of God moved upon the face of the waters (Gen. 1:2).
> Cast me not away from thy presence; and take not thy holy spirit from me (Ps. 51 :11).
> Whither shall I go from thy spirit? or whither shall I flee from thy presence? (Ps. 139:7).

Perhaps the clearest Old Testament presentation of the Trinity is given by the prophet Isaiah. In the forty-eighth chapter of this prophecy the Creator, who calls himself "the first and the last," speaks about the "Lord God and his Spirit." It is, without question, a description of Christ speaking about the Father and the Holy Spirit.

> Hearken unto me, O Jacob and Israel, my called; I am he; I am the first, I also am the last. [See Rev. 1:11.] Mine hand also hath laid the foundation of the earth, and my right hand hath spanned the heavens: when I call unto them, they stand up together. All ye, assemble yourselves, and hear; which among them hath declared these things? The Lord hath loved him: he will do his pleasure on Babylon, and his arm shall be on the Chaldeans. I, even I, have spoken; yea, I have called him: I have brought him, and he shall make his way prosperous. Come ye near unto me, hear ye this; I have not spoken in secret from the beginning; *from the time that it was, there am I: and now the Lord God, and his Spirit, hath sent me* (Isa. 48:12–16).

In the New Testament, also, truth about the Trinity is presented plainly.

The baptism of Jesus (Matt. 3:16–17) involves all three Persons of the Trinity.

The Father speaks from heaven.

The Son is baptized in the river Jordan.

The Holy Spirit descends in the form of a dove.

The Great Commission of Matthew 28:19 presents the Trinity as a plurality in unity. "Go ye, therefore, and teach all nations, baptizing them in the name [singular] of the Father, and of the Son, and of the Holy Ghost."

Paul's benediction at the close of his second letter to the church at Corinth allows us to know the thinking of the great apostle on this subject. He ends that letter asking the blessing of the Trinity upon the Corinthian believers. "The grace of the Lord Jesus Christ, and the love of God, and the communion of the Holy Ghost be with you all. Amen" (II Cor. 13:14).

So then we have seen, from the Scriptures of the Old and New Testaments, that the doctrine of the Holy Trinity is not pagan, but proper.

For additional study on the subject of the Trinity, I suggest the following:

> *The Trinity* by William E. Biederwolf—Eerdmans, Grand Rapids, Michigan.
> *The Secret of the Universe* by Nathan R. Wood—Eerdmans
> *The Great Doctrines of the Bible* by William Evans—Moody Press, Chicago, Illinois
> *The Trinity in the Old Testament*
> Tract by Morris Zutrau—The Friends of Israel Missionary Society (Spearhead Press), West Collingswood, New Jersey
> *The Trinity in the Old Testament*
> Tract by Milton B. Lindberg—American Messianic Fellowship, Chicago, Illinois

Chapter 8

WILL HERBERT W. ARMSTRONG BECOME GOD?

Herbert W. Armstrong believes that he will ultimately become God!

It sounds incredible, but it is true! And that is only part of the story.

He also has promised his followers that they have the opportunity to become God. He regards this as the very purpose for which we have been born. In his booklet *Why Were You Born?* he asks: "Do you really grasp it? The PURPOSE of your being alive is that finally you be BORN into the Kingdom of God, when you will actually BE GOD, even as Jesus was and is God, and His Father, a different Person, also is God!" (page 21).

Who can out-promise the former advertising man? Some church groups promise heaven, while others point to an earthly kingdom, or both, but who can compete with Armstrong's goal of actually becoming God? The devil stopped short of Armstrong's offer. He suggested to Eve that by eating the fruit of the tree of knowledge of good and evil she would be "as God" (Genesis 3:5, New Scofield). That doesn't measure up to Armstrong's claim.

Now, when will this great transformation from man to God take place? Armstrong expects to become God at the time of the resurrection. He explains:

The PURPOSE of life is that in us God is really re-creating *His own kind—reproducing Himself* after *His* own kind—for we are, upon real conversion, actually *begotten* as sons (yet unborn) of God; then through study of God's revelation in His Word, living by His every Word, constant prayer, daily experience with trials and testings, we grow spiritually more and more like God, until, at the time of the resurrection we shall be instantaneously CHANGED from mortal into *immortal*—we shall then be BORN of God—WE SHALL THEN BE GOD!" (*Why Were You Born?,* page 21).

He further informs his followers: "You are setting out on a training to become CREATOR—to become GOD!" (*Why Were You Born?,* page 22).

It cannot be stressed too much that Armstrong is not here telling his followers that they will become "gods," or even "Gods," but that they will actually become GOD.

Herbert Armstrong's error here stems primarily from his own misunderstanding of God. It seems fair to say that in his rejection of the Holy Spirit as a divine Person of the Trinity he has, in effect, moved himself and all true converts to the Worldwide Church of God into the position traditionally recognized as belonging to the Holy Spirit. (This is not to say that his position on the Father and the Son is correct.)

A clue to the Armstrong reasoning along this line is found in the following quotation from the article, "The God Family Open or Closed." There he has written: "*God is a Family*—not a trinity. God's Family will not be limited to an intractably closed circle of three. This is one group you don't have to be excluded from!" (*Tomorrow's World,* September–October 1970, page 31).

With this background, then, it is not surprising to find David Jon Hill waxing eloquent on the subject with statements that he admits some would reject as blasphemy. He equates the rejection of the doctrine that man can become God, with the rejection of the truth that Jesus Christ is the Son of God. He makes the following comparison:

> That God *could* become a human being, subject to death, subject to all of the manifold temptations of physical man (as Christ was) was and is totally unacceptable to Jewish thinking—so they rejected outright the claim of Jesus of Nazareth that He *was* the Son of God. Now, before you judge that rejection too harshly, let us remember that the vast majority of those who call themselves Christian reject outright as blasphemy and consider unthinkable the fact that human beings can become God! So we have on the one hand a great body of people who deny that God can become man and, on the other hand, a greater body of people who deny that man can become God! (*Tomorrow's World,* September–October 1970, page 25).

Mr. Hill does not hesitate to declare the degree of divinity that he expects to attain. He boasts:

> But at the time of the resurrection—when the promise of God the Father comes to pass and we are born from the grave—when our mortality puts on immortality and our corruption puts on incorruption—when we are changed from flesh to spirit and we become the living Sons of the Living God—when we become GOD AS GOD IS GOD, GOD AS JESUS CHRIST IS GOD—THEN WE will be able to see Jesus Christ just like He really is in all His spiritual splendor and glory! (*Tomorrow's World,* September–October 1970, page 28).

Neither is this doctrine considered optional for Armstrong's followers. It is labeled as "central, vital Bible truth," and Hill questions his readers about the reliability of their ministers whom he suspects are not preaching this same message. He asks: "Has your minister preached this central, vital Bible Truth? Have you heard before that your destiny is to become GOD AS GOD IS GOD?"

(*Tomorrow's World,* September–October 1970, page 28).

Unless Mr. Hill's readers are members of The Worldwide Church of God, it is fairly safe to say that they will have to give a negative answer to the above question. His position is so far from the historic Biblical concept of God that it would be difficult to find any minister other than a Mormon preaching this particular doctrine, and even their view is not identical.

Now what is it that has caused Herbert Armstrong to go so far afield in his understanding of what the Christian·will become at the resurrection? It is his erroneous understanding of the unity of the Godhead. To him the relationship between the Father and the Son is no more complex than that of an earthly family. He has written of Christ: "He is very God, even as God, the Father, is God. Yes, and Garner Ted is 'Armstrong,' even as I, his human father, am 'Armstrong' " (*Why Marriage! . . . Soon Obsolete?,* page 30).

Very simply then, he believes that this divine Family, made up of the Father and the Son, is God (See Chapter 7 on the Trinity), and that at the resurrection everyone who is "born" into this divine Family also becomes God.

Armstrong also defines God as a "kingdom." Under the heading "What Is the Kingdom of God?" he tries to make it plain to his readers:

> Jesus taught that WE, also, may be born into the God Family, which is the Kingdom of God, as we shall make plain.
>
> The God Family is also the God KINGDOM.
>
> Let's make that clear:
>
> One of the kingdoms in the world today is the Turkish nation. The Turkish people are the descendants of Esau. They are the FAMILY of Esau, twin brother of Jacob, grown into a nation—a kingdom.
>
> "Elohim" is the divine FAMILY. But "In the beginning Elohim *created.* . ." (Gen. 1:1). The God Family is the CREATOR Family. And God RULES over His creation. God's

throne, in heaven (Rev. 3:21, Isa. 66:1) is the seat of the Government of the Universe!

So the God Family is the Universe–Ruling Family—a Family which RULES—which *governs*—which is therefore a GOVERNMENT—and therefore also a KINGDOM—the Highest Kingdom.

When Jesus came teaching about the Kingdom of GOD, He was talking about the Family of God, and how WE humans, through Him, may be *born into it!*

Jesus taught: "Except a man be *born again,* he cannot see the kingdom of God" (John 3:3). God IS that Kingdom. God is composed of Spirit (John 4:24). Humans cannot SEE spirit. We cannot SEE God. Since God IS the Kingdom of God, human eyes cannot SEE that Kingdom (*Why Marriage! . . . Soon Obsolete?*, pages 32–33).

As to the future state, he adds:

. . . and therefore we *are,* now, material flesh. But when born *again,* next time born of the Spirit—which Spirit is God—we shall then *be* Spirit, even as God is Spirit—no longer flesh and blood (*Why Marriage! . . . Soon Obsolete?*, page 33).

In summary then, Mr. Armstrong believes that at the resurrection he and other converts will become God, as the Father is God and as the Son is God, and that they will be composed only of spirit, making it impossible for them to be seen by human eyes.

Now, enough of this speculation! Let us see what the Bible says about the state and substance of the saved after the resurrection.

First, let us be clear that while the Christian does have a wonderful future as a resurrected, glorified saint, he does not become God, or attain a position equal to that of Jesus Christ. The following verses prove that Christ is eternally superior to his creation:

And what is the exceeding greatness of his power to us-ward who believe, according to the working of his mighty power, which he wrought in Christ, when he raised him from the dead, and set him at his own right hand in the heavenly places, far above all principality and power, and might, and dominion, and every name that is named, *not only in this world, but also in that which is to come:* and hath put all things under his feet, and gave him to be the head over all things to the church, which is his body, the fulness of him that filleth all in all (Eph. 1:19–23).

Wherefore God also hath highly exalted him, and given him a name which is above every name: that at the name of Jesus every knee should bow, of things in heaven, and things in earth, and things under the earth; and that every tongue should confess that Jesus Christ is Lord, to the glory of God the Father (Phil. 2:9–11).

Scenes from heaven, after the first resurrection, describe those who have been redeemed by the blood of Christ as "kings and priests," but never as "God." Instead, in the book of Revelation, John tells of their worship and praise of God.

And they sung a new song, saying, Thou art worthy to take the book, and to open the seals thereof: for thou wast slain, and hast redeemed us to God by thy blood out of every kindred, and tongue, and people, and nation; and hast made us unto our God kings and priests: and we shall reign on the earth. . . . And every creature which is in heaven, and on the earth, and under the earth, and such as are in the sea, and all that are in them, heard I saying, Blessing, and honour, and glory, and power, be unto him that sitteth upon the throne, and unto the Lamb for ever and ever (Rev. 5:9–10, 13).

Near the end of that book, John writes that those who have had part in the first resurrection are "blessed and holy" and he calls them "priests of God and of Christ," but he never sees them exalted to the position of "becoming God."

Here is proof: "Blessed and holy is he that hath part in the first resurrection: on such the second death hath no power, but they shall be priests of God and of Christ, and shall reign with him a thousand years" (Rev. 20:6).

Second, the Bible teaches that the Christian will be resurrected *in his body,* rather than becoming, as Armstrong claims, a spirit which is God.

Job declared: "For I know that my redeemer liveth, and that he shall stand at the latter day upon the earth: and though after my skin worms destroy this body, yet in my flesh shall I see God: whom I shall see for myself, and mine eyes shall behold, and not another; though my reins be consumed within me" (Job 19:25-27).

David wrote of the resurrection of his "flesh" with confidence: "Therefore my heart is glad, and my glory rejoiceth: *my flesh also shall rest in hope*" (Ps. 16:9).

Paul assured the saints at Rome that the same power that raised Jesus from the dead would bring about their bodily resurrection. He explained: "But if the Spirit of him that raised up Jesus from the dead dwell in you, he that raised up Christ from the dead shall also quicken your mortal bodies by his Spirit that dwelleth in you" (Rom. 8:11).

He further instructed them that redemption includes the redemption of the body. "And not only they, but ourselves also, which have the firstfruits of the Spirit, even we ourselves groan within ourselves, waiting for the adoption, to wit, the redemption of our body" (Rom. 8:23).

Third, our resurrection will be similar to the resurrection of Christ. In His resurrection Christ is described as the "firstfruits" of them that slept (I Cor. 15:20). While the Bible *does not* teach that we will become God, as Herbert Armstrong wrongly expounds, it *does* teach that our resurrection body will be *like* the body of Jesus.

> For our conversation is in heaven; from whence also we look for the Saviour, the Lord Jesus Christ: who shall change our vile body, that it may be fashioned like unto his glorious body, according to the working whereby he is able even to subdue all things unto himself (Phil. 3:20–21).
>
> Beloved, now are we the sons of God, and it doth not yet appear what we shall be: but we know that, when he shall appear, we shall be like him; for we shall see him as he is (I John 3:2).

It is evident then that whatever we can learn about the resurrected body of Jesus we can expect to be true of our bodies when we are resurrected. The following verses tell of a meeting that Jesus had with His disciples after His resurrection.

> And as they thus spake, Jesus himself stood in the midst of them, and saith unto them, Peace be unto you. But they were terrified and affrighted, and supposed that they had seen a spirit. And he said unto them, Why are ye troubled? and why do thoughts arise in your hearts? Behold my hands and my feet, that it is I myself: handle me, and see; for a spirit hath not flesh and bones, as ye see me have. And when he had thus spoken, he shewed them his hands and his feet. And while they yet believed not for joy, and wondered, he said unto them, Have ye here any meat? And they gave him a piece of a broiled fish, and of an honeycomb. And he took it, and did eat before them (Luke 24:36–43).

A reading of Mr. Armstrong's material concerning the resurrection gives me the feeling that he is still under the same illusion that the doubting disciples experienced, as described in the above verses. They thought they saw a spirit! Mr. Armstrong has built his doctrine of the resurrection as if the disciples *had seen* a spirit. Remember, in writing of the coming resurrection, he has concluded:

" . . . we shall then *be* Spirit" (*Why marriage! . . . Soon Obsolete?*, page 33).

Notice now how Jesus dispelled that error from the minds of his disciples:

1. He urged them to "handle" His body to see that He was not a spirit (Luke 24:39).

2. He told them that His body was composed of "flesh and bones" and assured them that a spirit would not be composed of such solid substance (Luke 24:39).

3. He demonstrated the ability of His resurrection body to consume food. He ate broiled fish and honeycomb before them (Luke 24:42).

So, the Christian may anticipate the resurrection, in which his body will be like the body of Jesus. While it will be "spiritual" (I Cor. 15:44) it will not be "spirit" (Luke 24:39), but will perfectly equip him to reign with Christ in His kingdom (Rev. 20:6). He will not become "God," as Herbert Armstrong has erroneously promised to his followers, but he will enjoy the fellowship of his Lord, whose "name is above every name," forever (Phil. 2:9).

Chapter 9

HERBERT W. ARMSTRONG: CRUSADER AGAINST PAGANISM IN CHRISTMAS AND EASTER

Herbert W. Armstrong says a lot of things about Christmas and Easter that need to be said.

He asks the searching question that some preachers never ask, "What do Rudolph's red nose and eggnog have to do with Christmas?"

He blasts the commercialism of Christmas, and pens some words about gift giving that would make good advice for most of us in the Christmas season.

In his booklet *The Plain Truth About Christmas!* he zeroes in on gift trading to the exclusion of Christ, as follows:

Suppose someone you love has a birthday. You want to honor that person on his or her birthday. Would you lavishly buy gifts for *everyone else,* trading gifts back and forth with all your *other* friends and loved ones, but IGNORE COMPLETELY any gift for the one whose birthday you are honoring? Rather absurd, when viewed in that light, isn't it?

Yet this is exactly what people the world over are doing! . . . But I can say by years of experience, as I believe most pastors and ministers can say, that when the month of December rolls around, nearly all professing Christians forget to give gifts to CHRIST and HIS CAUSE almost altogether! December often is the most difficult month to keep CHRIST'S work from dying! People are too busy TRADING gifts back and forth among themselves to think of HIM and HIS WORK, it seems. Then in January and even into February it seems they have to catch up from what they spent for Christmas, so they seldom get back to normal in supporting CHRIST AND HIS WORK before March!

Now, of course, we understand that Armstrong's writings identify the work of Christ as synonymous with the work of The Worldwide Church of God, but we must admit that the criticism made in his article is too often true.

Garner Ted Armstrong heads his article on Easter with the title: "Lent, Ashes, Easter, Rabbits, and Eggs—What's it all about?"

> Just what *do* eggs have to do with Christ, and His resurrection? What DO rabbits and eggs have in common? Rabbits most assuredly *do not* lay eggs—even though millions of little children are taught to assume they *do!* (*The Plain Truth,* April 1965, page 45).

Who can deny the truth of Garner Ted's statement? Certainly the Armstrongs have a number of strong points in this area! Yet the wise reader will get the whole picture, for while there is some correct criticism, there is also dangerous error.

For example, if one is not careful, this great smoke-screen of complaint about many of the customs of Christmas will cover up Armstrong's very serious mistake about the incarnation of Christ.

Vital to an appreciation of the Incarnation is the fact that this One born in the stable is none other than God Himself, in the person of His Son. In other words, Jesus Christ was "the image of the invisible God" (Col. 1:15).

The writer of the book of Hebrews describes the relationship of the incarnate Christ to the Godhead as follows:

God, who at sundry times and in divers manners spake in time past unto the fathers by the prophets, hath in these last days spoken unto us by his Son, whom he hath appointed heir of all things, by whom also he made the worlds; who being the brightness of his glory, and *the express image of his person,* and upholding all things by the word of his power, when he had by himself purged our sins, sat down on the right hand of the Majesty on high (Heb. 1:1–3).

The importance of a correct understanding of this fact cannot be overstated because it is an inseparable part of the reconciling work of God that makes salvation possible. Paul declares:

Therefore if any man be in Christ, he is a new creature: old things are passed away; behold, all things are become new. And all things are of God, who hath reconciled us to himself by Jesus Christ, and hath given to us the ministry of reconciliation; to wit, that *God was in Christ* reconciling the world unto himself, not imputing their trespasses unto them; and hath committed unto us the word of reconciliation. (II Cor. 5:17–19).

Simply stated then, the Incarnation was God *in* Christ, not just *represented by* Christ as a member of His "Family."

It is here that the gap in Armstrong's understanding of God is most evident, for having rejected the doctrine of the Trinity he concludes that God is simply a Family, just like an earthly family. He explains:

Jesus was born, by the resurrection, as the divine Son of GOD, with divine POWER. He who had been *born human*—who had died—was born again—by a resurrection into the very divine GOD FAMILY. He is ONE *with* God. He *is* very GOD, even as God, the Father, is God.

Yes, and Garner Ted is "Armstrong," even as I, his human father, am "Armstrong." I am human; Garner Ted, begotten of me, was born human. God is divine; Jesus, begotten of Him, was born divine by a resurrection (*Why Marriage!*

. . Soon Obsolete?, page 30).

The truth is, then, that in denying Jesus Christ is the second Person of the *Trinity*, Herbert Armstrong does more injustice to the Bible account of the birth of Christ than do all the "pagan" customs that he attacks.

Likewise, his accurate observations concerning some of the practices of our present-day Easter observances seem relatively unimportant when weighed against his monumental error about the resurrection itself. It is in this area, where the Armstrongs are slicing right and left at others, that they have, themselves, stumbled into one of their most serious errors.

Let me illustrate.

In the article "Why Celebrate Easter?" by Eugene M. Walter, the Armstrong doctrine of the resurrection is set forth as sensationally as it might have been by Herbert W. himself.

Proving that he has been a good pupil of Armstrong's journalistic style, Mr. Walter declares:

> Shocking though it may be, either the "Good Friday–Easter Sunday" tradition is a *fable*—or you have *no Saviour!* Jesus gave only *one sign* to prove that He was the Messiah. That sign was the *length of time He would be dead and buried.*
>
> Notice Jesus' own words concerning this ONLY SIGN that would prove His Messiahship:
>
> "An evil and adulterous generation seeketh after a sign; and there shall no sign be given to it, but the sign of the prophet Jonas: for as Jonas was three days and three nights in the whale's belly; so shall the Son of man be three days and three nights in the heart of the earth" (Matt. 12:39–40).
>
> Did Christ *mean what He said?* Did He really *expect* to be buried in the earth for three days and three nights—a full 72 hours? (*The Plain Truth*, March 1966, page 30).

Now we have no argument with Mr. Armstrong, nor

his writers, in demanding that Christ be in the grave a full seventy-two hours, or three days and three nights. In fact, there are *many* scholarly Christians who have *long* believed that Jesus was crucified on a Wednesday rather than the traditional Friday. (See *Difficulties in the Bible* by R. A. Torrey, published by Moody Press.)

What is missed, however, in the above article, is the fact that Jesus not only revealed the exact length of time that He would be in the grave, but also that He would be resurrected in the same body that was crucified.

> Jesus answered and said unto them, Destroy this temple, and in three days I will raise it up. Then said the Jews, Forty and six years was this temple in building, and wilt thou rear it up in three days? But he spake of the temple of his body (John 2:19–21).

It is at this point that Herbert Armstrong falters. Under the heading "Not Resurrected in Same Body" he mistakenly insists: "Now notice carefully. God the Father did not cause Jesus Christ to get back into the body which had died" (*Tomorrow's World*, March–April 1970, page 7).

Mr. Armstrong does not bother to tell us what happened to the body of Jesus that had been laid in the tomb, but Dr. C. Paul Meredith, one of his writers, simply says that it disappeared! (*If You Die . . . Will You Live Again?*, page 2).

Shades of doubting Thomas! Here is error more deadly than all the Easter-bunny stories.

Not only had Jesus assured His disciples of this coming resurrection, but the prophet Zechariah had predicted that the faithful in Israel would look upon the very wounds of the risen and returning Lord.

> And I will pour upon the house of David, and upon the inhabitants of Jerusalem, the spirit of grace and of supplica-

tions: and they shall look upon me whom they have pierced . . . (Zech. 12:10).

And one shall say unto him, What are these wounds in thine hands? Then he shall answer, Those with which I was wounded in the house of my friends (Zech. 13:6).

After the resurrection Jesus seemed especially anxious to guard the disciples against the very error that Mr. Armstrong is propagating, for He invited them to carefully examine His hands and feet where the wounds had been made and then to further demonstrate that He was not a spirit He ate fish and honeycomb before them (Luke 24:39–42).

Furthermore, His conversation with Thomas indicates that acceptance of anything less than the bodily resurrection is the very opposite of faith, without which it is impossible to please God (Heb. 11:6).

Then said he to Thomas, Reach hither thy finger, and behold my hands; and reach hither thy hand, and thrust it into my side: and be not *faithless,* but believing. And Thomas answered and said unto him, My Lord and my God. Jesus saith unto him, Thomas, because thou hast seen me, thou hast believed: blessed are they that have not seen, and yet have believed (John 20:27–29).

So the champion who seemed to promise to lead us through the maze of paganism to the pure truth has failed again, and under the careful scrutiny of God's Word has been weighed in the balances and found wanting.

Meanwhile, as Herbert W. Armstrong pursues the origins of paganistic practices, and the world rushes on in mad commercialism, a few sincere Christians here and there worship the living Christ who was born in Bethlehem's stable . . . and the Lord warms their hearts with His blessing.

Chapter 10

HERBERT W. ARMSTRONG'S SURPRISING STAND ON ALCOHOL AND WORLDLINESS

I have met very few people who are aware of the Armstrong position on alcoholic beverages and worldliness. Those with whom I have become acquainted who *do* understand it have learned almost entirely from *first-hand experience,* and are now completely disillusioned with the whole movement.

With Armstrong's emphasis on works and law keeping, most people just seem to take for granted that his stand on these issues must naturally follow that pattern. They have trouble believing the truth about his liberal views in this practical area.

It is my opinion that Armstrong is aware that his teaching on this subject would "turn off" thousands of his listeners and readers who are now Christians, and that is why so little has been written in *The Plain Truth* promoting his position.

I have been gathering material on Armstrongism for fifteen years, and I have before me only one copy of an article revealing his views on such things as dancing, card playing, drinking, etc. It is entitled "What Is Worldliness?" and is published in the September 1969 issue of *Tomorrow's World*. It is written by Mr. Roderick C. Meredith.

The opening paragraphs of the article ooze with sarcasm. Evidently Mr. Meredith has in mind someone who has the reputation of being a dedicated Christian and abstains from some things that Meredith thinks are permissible. He cuts him down with an avalanche of adjectives! I quote:

> CAN YOU be a *completely dedicated* Christian without being some kind of "freak"?
> Without missing out on the interest and excitement of our fast-moving jet age? Without appearing sanctimonious or "nicey nice" and talking a lot of religious gobbledegook?
> . . . Don't take your former opinion—*or any opinion*—for granted. Learn to *think*—to carefully *meditate* and consider the *end result* of each course of action in broadest terms—and to PROVE what your Creator says in His inspired Bible!
> If you do, you will find that the great Creator of this vast universe is NOT a "pin-headed," small-minded, old fuddy-duddy type or creaky great grandfather figure at all. He is not trying to "catch" people in some little act He arbitrarily defines as "sinful."

Even our forefathers, and the godly pioneer preachers, do not escape Meredith's attack on those who choose the separated life. Of them he has written:

> And although the "old-fashioned gospel" preachers of a bygone puritanical Protestant era invented the idea that drinking, dancing, card playing, and theater-going were "worldly," we have seen that they are NOT wrong at all if used *in the proper manner.*

Without a doubt, the greatest danger springing from Mr. Meredith's article is his condoning of the use of alcoholic beverages. This coming from a man writing in a religious publication has the potential of starting numbers of people drinking who otherwise might never have begun. Indeed, Meredith seems to think that " . . . weak character is the result if one does not indulge in at least some drinking." He explains:

> Nevertheless, God gave us wine and alcoholic beverages to learn to use *properly*—and to develop CHARACTER by the proper exercise of *wisdom* and *self-control*. *Prohibition* is NOT God's way—and it does *not* develop character (pages 25–26).

Let me tell you about a family that experienced the results of Mr. Meredith's suggested Character Building Course.

These people came from another state to counsel with me about their son. They knew that I had made a study of Armstrongism and they were heartbroken because their son had accepted the teachings of The Worldwide Church of God.

This young man had first begun to hear Mr. Armstrong on the radio, and then had rented a post office box so that he could receive *The Plain Truth* and other publications without his parents knowing about it.

By the time the parents were aware of what was happening, their son had accepted, completely, the doctrines of Armstrongism, including the teaching that alcoholic beverages were perfectly all right when used in moderation.

Moderation with alcohol, however, is often one thing to write about and quite another to achieve. Authorities tell us that of ten people who start to use alcohol, three will become addicted to it. Witness the fact that today there are between six and seven million alcoholics in the United States, while probably most of that number intended to use alcohol only moderately.

When the young man became old enough to buy alcoholic beverages he began to drink with some of the men at his place of employment. After all, his new religion did not urge total abstinence from alcoholic beverages.

Soon, however, he could not control his desire, and began to drink too much.

One day, while intoxicated, he was involved in a serious accident which necessitated the amputation of one of his legs.

Now, as I recall that tragic story, I think how wise it would have been for Mr. Meredith to have followed his own advice: "Learn to think—to carefully meditate and consider the end result of each course of action in broadest terms . . . ."

Perhaps it would have been helpful for Roderick Meredith and his friends to have sat with me to hear about the "end result" of their teaching.

In contrast to Mr. Meredith's views, consider the good advice in the book of Proverbs:

> Wine is a mocker, strong drink is raging: and whosoever is decieved thereby is not wise (Prov. 20:1).
> Who hath woe? who hath sorrow? who hath contentions? who hath babbling? who hath wounds without cause? who hath redness of eyes? They that tarry long at the wine; they that go to seek mixed wine. Look not thou upon the wine when it is red, when it giveth his colour in the cup, when it moveth itself aright. At the last it biteth like a serpent, and stingeth like an adder (Prov. 23:29–32).

Certainly Paul's instruction as to things lawful applies to the use of alcohol. "All things are lawful unto me, but all things are not expedient: all things are lawful for me, but I will not be brought under the power of any" (I Cor. 6:12).

By its very nature, alcohol immediately begins to bring the user under its power, and the Christian will be wise to avoid its use, Mr. Meredith's prescription for strong character notwithstanding.

So, now the Armstrong attitude on worldliness and

drinking is made public again! Here we have seen proof of the position of The Worldwide Church of God on this subject, from their own publication. This is not hearsay!

What then should be the Christian's response? Should he be a listener to *The World Tomorrow?* Should he receive *The Plain Truth* as a good news-magazine, and hope to be able to sort out truth from error? Should he support the Armstrong position on worldliness and alcohol?

Certainly not!

The Christian's course of action is made clear in the Scriptures: "Wherefore come out from among them, and be ye separate, saith the Lord, and *touch not the unclean thing;* and I will receive you, and will be a Father unto you, and ye shall be my sons and daughters, saith the Lord Almighty" (II Cor. 6:17–18).

With the abundance of excellent Bible-centered literature, and outstanding Christian radio ministries available today, there is no reason for the sincere Christian to expose himself to the errors of Armstrongism.

Chapter 11

YOUR QUESTIONS ANSWERED

Since the publication of my earlier analysis of Armstrongism, entitled *Herbert W. Armstrong: Mr. Confusion,* I have had mail from many countries of the world from people seeking additional information about these strange doctrines.

In the preceeding chapters I have tried to enlarge upon the areas where the Armstrongs have the most significant errors in Bible interpretation.

In addition to the material already given, I now include six questions that have appeared to be uppermost in the minds of those who have written, called, or who have come in person to find the way from CONFUSION to Bible truth.

QUESTION:

If Herbert W. Armstrong is so confused, how did he know twenty-five or thirty years ago that there would be a United States of Europe?

ANSWER:

The teaching of a union of nations in Europe is by no means original with Herbert W. Armstrong. Students of the prophetic scriptures have been predicting the revival of the Roman Empire for many years. In his book *Lectures on Daniel,* published in 1911, Dr. H. A. Ironside wrote about this, as did many others before the era of Armstrongism.

QUESTION:

How can you believe in an everlasting hell when Malachi 4:1–3 tells us that the saints will walk in the ashes of the wicked?

ANSWER:

To apply Malachi 4:1–3 to the Bible doctrine of hell or eternal punishment would be taking it entirely out of context. This portion of Scripture has nothing to do with the souls or spirits of men but refers to the physical death of the wicked at the second coming of Christ.

QUESTION:

Where is there a mention in the Bible of man's immortal soul?

ANSWER:

There is a great deal of scripture having to do with the conscious existence after death of both the saved and the lost. It is true that the words "immortal soul," used as such, do not appear in the Bible. It is also true that the term "millennium" does not appear in the Bible, yet Herbert Armstrong does not reject the teaching concerning the millennium and in fact has written a lengthy article "Where Will the Millennium Be Spent?" It is then inconsistent for him to reject the true Bible teaching of man's existence after death on the basis that the words "immortal soul" are not to be found in the Bible.

The words of Jesus in Luke 16:19–31 give a fearful glimpse into hell where the wicked rich man is able to hear, see, feel pain, and speak. The appearance of Elijah and Moses on the mount of transfiguration gives evidence that the righteous are in a conscious state after leaving this earthly scene. Multiplied statements of the Apostle Paul make clear the fact that Christians who die are immediately "with the Lord." Examples are: Philippians 1:19–21, II Corinthians 5:1–10, II Timothy 4:6–8, and I Thessalonians 4:14.

Herbert W. Armstrong rejects the teaching that the individual is in a conscious existence after physical death in an effort to escape the true Bible teaching on the destiny of the lost in hell and of the saved in heaven. Like the Jehovah's Witnesses, one of his proof verses for this teaching is Ezekiel 18:4: "The soul that sinneth, it shall die."

What Armstrong carefully avoids in order to protect his "no eternal punishment" teaching is the truth that spiritual death does not mean the cessation of existence. For example, before a man is saved, he is spiritually dead according to Ephesians 2:1, yet he does not cease to exist, nor does he lose control of his physical capabilities.

If Ezekiel 18:4 teaches eternal death for the sinner, it certainly would apply to the "man of sin" of II Thessalonians 2:3, who is yet to come upon the world scene. Yet, according to Revelation 20:10, which gives us a preview of the eternal doom of this individual, he has not ceased to exist even after one thousand years in the "lake of fire." The verse is plain: "And the devil that deceived them was cast into the lake of fire and brimstone, where the beast and the false prophet are, and shall be tormented day and night for ever and ever."

The Bible definition of "life" is to know Christ (John 17:3). The Bible definition of "death" is to be separated from Him.

QUESTION:

Is it not wrong to celebrate Christmas since it is so paganized?

ANSWER:

There is certainly much about the way the world celebrates Christmas that is wrong in God's sight. However, we must face the fact that the world has misused nearly everything that Christians hold sacred, including the Bible, gospel music, the Lord's Day, and much more. If we were to discard everything that the world has adapted to its own purpose, we would have nothing left.

The truth is that thousands of Christians find real blessing in remembering the birth of Christ at Christmas. The Lord knows the heart that is truly thankful for all that is involved in the humiliation and incarnation of Christ at His birth in Bethlehem. No good purpose is served in persuading people to stop setting aside a special time to worship and praise God for Christ's coming to save us.

If your Christmas can pass the test of Colossians 3:17, it will not be wrong for you to celebrate. "And whatsoever ye do in word or deed, do all in the name of the Lord Jesus, giving thanks to God and the Father by him." For further information, see Chapter 9.

QUESTION:

How can Herbert Armstrong continue as he does without asking for money, if his work is not of God?

ANSWER:

It is true that Mr. Armstrong does not charge for his pamphlets, nor is there a subscription price for his magazine *The Plain Truth*. You are reminded of this fact in nearly every issue.

There are at least two factors that make it possible for him to continue this practice.

The first is that many people send gifts when writing for free material from a religious work. This is a fact which you may investigate by writing any religious broadcaster.

The second and greater reason, however, is that Herbert Armstrong presents his work as the only one worthy of tithes and offerings. In this he is unlike many other religious broadcasters who expect, and sometimes even urge, you to support your local church, and then send additional gifts to assist in their work. Armstrong believes the message your church proclaims is a "Satanic counterfeit" instead of the message of Christ, and is therefore not worthy of your support. Once you become convinced of that, the next natural step is to send all of your tithes and offerings to The Worldwide Church of God.

It is also to be noted that while Mr. Armstrong is willing to send his literature free to those who request it, he is not nearly as easy-going in money matters with his followers as the public might think.

I have a letter written by him from the Ambassador College in England on September 26, 1969. The letter reveals that Mr. Armstrong is very concerned about attempts to link his work with an arsonist charged with setting fire to the Al Aksa Mosque. He informs his readers that defense of these accusations is costing great effort and expense. He pleads:

> This month of September started out with good sums of tithes and offerings coming in—for a few days—and then slacked off! Please send in contributions AS OFTEN as possible—and keep it up during the last half of the month. The need is great, and serious and urgent.

Likewise, his letter of July 29, 1969 contains a call for money. Here he threatens:

> ONLY the income is lacking! We must get it back up! Otherwise I have to cancel about 100 radio stations and cut PLAIN TRUTH circulation in half. That would be an unthinkable tragedy. It would be DISASTROUS. But I will be forced to do just that unless income picks up! It's no "wolf-wolf cry"!

He concludes the letter urging his readers to "increase

the amount you send."

If you think that Armstrong makes no mention of financial needs to anyone, you simply do not have the facts, as these letters prove. These letters were furnished to me by families once affected by Armstrong's preaching.

QUESTION:
Where does the Bible mention Sunday as the Sabbath?
ANSWER:
Sunday is not the Sabbath. Saturday is the Sabbath, as given to Israel in the law of Moses. According to Colossians 2:14–17 the Sabbath days were a shadow for the Israelites of things to come, that were fulfilled in Christ.

> Let no man therefore judge you in meat, or in drink, or in respect of an holyday, or of the new moon, or of the sabbath days; which are a shadow of things to come; but the body is of Christ (Col. 2:16–17).

After the resurrection of Christ we find the early Christians meeting together on the first day of the week, or the Lord's Day, for the breaking of bread and the preaching of God's Word (Acts 20:7). Paul instructs the Corinthians that the first day of the week is the day for the laying aside of their offerings (I Cor. 16:2).

It was, without doubt, the practice of the early church to remember the resurrection of Christ on the first day of the week. Ignatius, Bishop of Antioch, in the year 110 A.D. wrote:

> Those who walked in the ancient practices attain unto newness of hope, no longer observing sabbaths, but fashioning their lives after the Lord's Day, on which our life also rose through Him, that we may be found disciples of Jesus Christ, our only Teacher.

In the mind of Herbert Armstrong, however, those

in the early church who did not observe the Sabbath on Saturday could not have been true Christians. To him, the keeping of the Sabbath determines whether one is to be saved or lost. In his book *Which Day Is the Christian Sabbath?* he calls Sabbath keeping "the TEST COMMAND—the one on which YOUR VERY SALVATION and ETERNITY DEPENDS!" (page 58).

It is significant that those who hold to the Sabbath as given to Israel usually hold also to a mixture of law and grace for the Christian today, often including the Old Testament dietary laws (see I Timothy 4:1–6) and sometimes, as is true with Armstrong, even the Jewish feasts.

Those who find themselves confused by Armstrong's legalism will find their questions answered in Paul's letter to the Galatians. Listed below are some excerpts from that epistle which deal especially with the problem of legalism.

> I do not frustrate the grace of God: for if righteousness come by the law, then Christ is dead in vain (Gal. 2:21).
> But before faith came, we were kept under the law, shut up unto the faith which should afterwards be revealed. Wherefore the law was our schoolmaster to bring us unto Christ, that we might be justified by faith. But after that faith is come, we are no longer under a schoolmaster. For ye are all the children of God by faith in Christ Jesus (Gal. 3:23–26).
> But now, after that ye have known God, or rather are known of God, how turn ye again to the weak and beggarly elements, whereunto ye desire again to be in bondage? Ye observe days, and months, and times, and years. I am afraid of you, lest I have bestowed upon you labour in vain (Gal. 4:9–11).

For further information and help on the question of legalism see the fourteenth chapter of Romans.

Also especially helpful on this subject is the book *The Gospel in the Feasts of Israel* by Victor Buksbazen. Information for securing the above mentioned book is given in Chapter 5.

As I have listened to Herbert W. Armstrong's broadcast "The World Tomorrow," read his tracts, and searched through his magazine *The Plain Truth*, I have concluded that this religious system might be called "The Religion of the Unreal." Heaven is not really a hope. Hell is not really hell. Grace is not really sufficient grace. Salvation is not in this life really salvation. The nation of Israel is not really Israel.

How refreshing it has been to hear of many who have left this system of error to return to real Bible truth and to give their talents and energies to the work of Christ in their local Bible-believing churches.

Perhaps your question is one of those listed above. Perhaps you will be the next to turn from the errors of Armstrongism to Bible truth.

"I have no greater joy than to hear that my children walk in truth" (III John 4).

Chapter 12

WE ESCAPED FROM ARMSTRONGISM

By Wayne Leyendecker
(as told to Roger F. Campbell)

Should we worship on Saturday instead of Sunday?
Are Americans really Israelites? Is it sinful to celebrate
Christmas? Should we change our eating habits? Are all
churches preaching lies except Herbert W. Armstrong's
Radio Church of God?*

These were a few of the questions that raced through
my mind and demanded answers when I became
interested in the dynamic radio preaching of Armstrong.

I first became interested in Herbert Armstrong when
some friends left their church and began to follow his
teachings. I became a regular listener to "The World
Tomorrow," as he titles his broadcast, and I awaited
eagerly each issue of *The Plain Truth* magazine.

Religion had not held much interest for me in the past.
Most of the religious matters of our family had been
left to Ruth, my wife. She had attended church since
she was a child and was now taking our three children
Rosalyn, Gary, and Michele to the River Bend Bible

---

*Herbert W. Armstrong's "Worldwide Church of God" was called
"The Radio Church of God" at the time of Mr. Leyendecker's conversion.

Church, a mission church which meets in a schoolhouse near our home.

As the weeks passed and my interest in Armstrongism increased, I began to see that there were serious conflicts between the teaching my family was receiving at the church, and that which was persuasively presented on Armstrong's broadcast and in his literature.

The church taught the doctrine of the Trinity, while Armstrong insisted this was pagan in its origin. Songs about heaven were a regular part of the worship services at the church, but *The Plain Truth* publications declared that heaven was not the reward of the saved. The church worshiped on Sunday, but the evidence presented by Herbert Armstrong seemed conclusive that Saturday was the proper day.

I pointed out these things to Ruth and the children. I called Ruth's attention to the authority with which Armstrong spoke, and we noted together the many Bible verses he presented as proof for his teachings. And there was the impressive number of unfolding world events that Armstrong neatly fitted into his prophetic teaching. Ruth was not fully convinced, but we decided to follow the teachings of Herbert W. Armstrong.

We began to keep Saturday as our day of rest and worship. We dropped all pork from our diet. We even considered driving weekly from our home near Grand Rapids, Michigan, to South Bend, Indiana, a distance of 100 miles, to attend a gathering of followers of the Radio Church of God.

Our decision to follow this new way of life was made near the Christmas season, and we decided there would be no recognition of Christmas at all, except for a few exchanges of gifts, since, according to Armstrong, all Christmas festivities are rooted in paganism. We sent no greeting cards to friends or relatives. We had no Christmas tree.

We must have been expecting a great blessing from that "no Christmas" experience, but instead it seemed barren and empty. We truly missed remembering Christ's birth that year.

Somehow, following the "Armstrong way of life" was not nearly as satisfying as I had anticipated. The conflicts within grew rather than subsided. Unanswered questions pressed upon my mind every waking hour. My work required me to be alert, but my inward struggles demanded priority. Every part of my life was affected by the awful uncertainty as to my relationship with God.

While I had little instruction in the Bible, I had always held a great respect for the Scriptures. The thought struck me that God must have the answer to my spiritual struggle, and that His answer must be contained in the Bible. I determined I would seek out the truth in the Bible, and that I would not rest until I had found peace with God.

It was about 5 o'clock in the evening when I opened my Bible to begin my search. I read with an urgency and interest greater than I had ever experienced. I read carefully and yet swiftly. It was as if I were trying to devour the whole Bible in an evening, and yet to sift from its pages some single truth that would be the key to this crisis in my life.

The hours passed quickly. That night I read for 11 hours, and when I closed the Bible at 4 o'clock in the morning it was only because my eyes were too weary to continue. At 7 o'clock I was awake and back to the Bible again. All through that next day I continued my study. It would have been useless for me to attempt to carry on the usual business of the day.

My Bible reading did not end until that evening. When I finally closed the Bible that evening, I still did not have the answer.

A few days later a business trip took me away from

the city. I had pulled myself together enough to carry on my work, but the struggle continued. On the return trip the battle within became more intense, and I brought my car to a stop beside the road and once again opened the Bible.

Nearly all of my Bible searching had been in the Old Testament. Much of what I had read had seemed to substantiate Armstrong's doctrines. God had indeed given instruction concerning the eating of meats, the keeping of feast days such as the Passover, the Feast of Tabernacles, and the Sabbath days, all of which Armstrong insists are to be kept today.

That cold winter day, however, as I sat in my car, the story of Christ and His love in the book of Matthew made a new impression upon my heart. As I finished the 28 chapters and resumed my journey home, I felt sure the end of my search was near. The following Sunday our family attended the River Bend Bible Church. I listened with interest to everything the pastor had to say that day. Many of his comments on the Bible called to my mind the picture of Christ's death that had been portrayed so clearly in my reading of Matthew's Gospel. Before we left the church, I invited the pastor to visit our home. I thought perhaps his knowledge of the Bible might enable him to help me.

A few years earlier, I might have been careful to avoid a meeting with the minister, but I awaited this visit of Pastor Wright Van Plew with real anticipation. I wondered if he would really have the answers.

When Pastor Van Plew arrived, I found that he had not come for a debate on Herbert Armstrong, but rather for my decision to trust Jesus Christ. Repeatedly he maneuvered the conversation from "questions" to "Christ."

I was brought to see that my real need was to receive

Jesus Christ by faith. This night in my home, I was able to see myself as a lost sinner in need of the living Saviour. I saw that my real need was not laws, but faith in the Son of God who loved me and gave Himself for me. I told Christ of my sin and I trusted Him as my personal Saviour.

After the pastor had given me verses of assurance from the Bible, he turned to Ruth and asked her how things were with her soul.

Ruth says now that in that moment she was angry and offended. After all, she had been brought up in church and had been trained in the teachings of the Bible since she was a child. She had taken the children to Sunday School and church services. Why should anyone question her salvation, even if she had yielded to some of her husband's wishes to follow the teachings of Herbert W. Armstrong?

Before the next Sunday arrived, however, Ruth also had realized her personal need of Christ. She is thankful now for that question that shocked her into the realization that even religious training does not guarantee salvation. She rejoices now in faith in her living Saviour.

Since Christ has come into our lives, our daily experience is truly much richer. There are ways in which we need to grow in Christ, but with His help we are determined to do that. We want to be so yielded to Christ that He will be able to use us in our local church to carry the message of salvation to others of our local community.

We are grateful to God that he guided us out of the errors of Armstrongism into the truth of Christ and His salvation. It was such a relief to find that all the demands of the law were fulfilled in Christ, but beyond that it has been wonderful to find that the demands of our hearts for peace and assurance are also fulfilled in Him.

INDEX OF BIBLE QUOTATIONS

Chapter 2

Page 19   Psalm 11:4
             Mark 13:32
     20   II Kings 2:1, 11
             Luke 15:7
             John 14:2
             Philippians 3:20; 1:21–23
     21   II Corinthians 5:6–8; 12:4
             I Peter 1:4
             Revelation 5:9–10
     22   Revelation 6:9–11

Chapter 3

Page 28   I Corinthians 12:12–13
     29   Ephesians 5:30, 32

Chapter 4

Page 33 I Corinthians 3:1–2

  35 Luke 1:24, 31, 36; 2:21

      Luke 1:57; 2:7, 11

      Matthew 1:21, 23, 25; 2:2

      John 16:21

      Revelation 12:2, 4, 5, 13

      Hebrews 11:11

      I Peter 1:23—2:2

  36 Ephesians 4:14–15

  37 Ephesians 5:18

      John 1:12–13; 3:1–16

      I John 5:1

      II Peter 3:18

Chapter 5

Page 40 I Corinthians 1:18

  41 John 5:24

      Ephesians 2:8

      Titus 3:5

      I John 5:12–13

  42 Colossians 2:16–17

      Galatians 3:1–3

  44 Hebrews 9:27

      Luke 16:22–23

  45 Matthew 28:18–20

II Peter 3:4–9
II Corinthians 6:2

Chapter 6

Page 51   Deuteronomy 1:10
              II Chronicles 1:9
      52   Deuteronomy 32:26–27
      54   Amos 9:8–9, 11–12, 15
              Ezra 7:7
              Nehemiah 7:73; 9:2
      55   Acts 2:36
              Luke 2:36
              John 1:47; 3:1, 10
              II Corinthians 11:22–23
              Acts 5:35
   55–56   Acts 26:4–7
      56   Matthew 10:5–7; 15:24
      58   Romans 11:25
      59   II Samuel 7:4–5, 12–16
      60   Psalms 132:11–12
              I Chronicles 28:6–7
              Hoseah 3:4
              Luke 1:32–33
      61   Genesis 28:22; 35:14
              Jeremiah 43:8–11
      62   Jeremiah 44:14, 28

Chapter 7

Page 69   John 16:7–8, 13–14
      70   Ephesians 4:30
              I Thessalonians 5:19
              Acts 5:3
              I Corinthians 2:10–11; 12:11
      71   Genesis 1:26; 3:22; 11:7
      72   Deuteronomy 6:4
              Numbers 13:23
              Malachi 1:6
              Isaiah 63:16
              Proverbs 30:4
              Psalms 2:7, 12
              Hebrews 1:5
      73   Genesis 1:2
              Psalms 51:11; 139:7
              Revelation 1:11
              Isaiah 48:12–16
              Matthew 3:16–17
      74   Matthew 28:19
              II Corinthians 13:14

Chapter 8

Page 80   Ephesians 1:19–23
              Philippians 2:9–11
              Revelation 5:9–10, 13

81	Revelation 20:6
	Job 19:25–27
	Psalms 16:9
	Romans 8:11, 23
	I Corinthians 15:20
82	Philippians 3:20–21
	I John 3:2
	Luke 24:36–43
83	Luke 24:39, 42
	I Corinthians 15:44
	Revelation 20:6
	Philippians 2:9

Chapter 9

Page 86	Colossians 1:15
87	Hebrews 1:1–3
	II Corinthians 5:17–19
89	John 2:19–21
89–90	Zechariah 12:10
90	Zechariah 13:6
	Luke 24:39–42
	Hebrews 11:6
	John 20:27–29

Chapter 10

Page 94	Proverbs 20:1; 23:29–32

94   I Corinthians 6:12
95   II Corinthians 6:17–18

Chapter 11

Page 98   Malachi 4:1–3
           Luke 16:19–31
           Philippians 1:19–21
           II Corinthians 5:1–10
           II Timothy 4:6–8
     99   I Thessalonians 4:14
           Ephesians 2:1
           Ezekiel 18:4
           II Thessalonians 2:3
           Revelation 20:10
           John 17:3
    100   Colossians 3:17
    102   Colossians 2:16–17
           Acts 20:7
           I Corinthians 16:2
    103   I Timothy 4:1–6
           Galatians 2:21; 3:23–26; 4:9–11
    104   III John 4

INDEX OF QUOTATIONS FROM ARMSTRONG MATERIAL

Chapter 1

Page 11   Letter to *The Plain Truth* subscribers.
     12   Letter to co-workers, Jan. 29, 1971.
     13   Booklet *The Autobiography of Herbert W. Armstrong*, page 35.
  13–14   *The Autobiography of Herbert W. Armstrong, Volume I*, pages 400, 407.
  14–15   *Ibid.*, pages 76–77.

Chapter 2

Page 18   "Will You Get to Heaven?" *The Plain Truth*, Oct. 1961, pages 16–17.
     19   "What is Man?" *The Plain Truth*, Mar. 1957, page 8.
     22   *The Plain Truth*, Feb. 1958, page 20.

Chapter 3

Page 24   "Why a Church?" *The Plain Truth*, Aug. 1962, page 43.
          "Here's Why the Word of God Is the Foundation of Knowledge," *Tomorrow's World*, May–June 1970, page 14.
     25   "How Would You Recognize the Church Jesus Founded?" *The Plain Truth*, June 1968, pages 42–43.

26   "Where Is the True Church Today?" *The Plain Truth*,
     Feb. 1958, page 23.
     "The True Church—Where Is It?" *The Plain Truth*,
     Mar. 1963, pages 44–45.
27   *The Autobiography of Herbert W. Armstrong, Volume I*,
     page 505.
     "A True History of the True Church," *The Plain
     Truth*, Jan. 1959, page 29.
28   *The Plain Truth*, Jan. 1959, page 3.

Chapter 4

Page 31   *Just What Do You Mean—Born Again?* page 3.
     32   *Why Were You Born?* page 13.
     33   *Just What Do You Mean—Born Again?* pages 7–8.
     34   *Why Marriage! . . . Soon Obsolete?* page 31.
     35   *Ibid.*, page 30.
     36   *Just What Do You Mean—Born Again?* page 11.

Chapter 5

Page 39   *Why Were You Born?* page 11.
   39–40 "Religious Revival in This Twentieth Century," *The
          Plain Truth*, Mar. 1957, page 12.
     40   "Please Don't Give Me That Old-Time Religion,"
          The Plain Truth, Feb. 1968, page 43.
     41   *What Do You Mean—Salvation?* page 21.
          "False Conversion," *The Plain Truth*, Oct. 1955 and
          Nov. 1966.
     42   *Which Day Is the Christian Sabbath?* page 58.
     43   *Predestination*, page 11.
     44   *Is This the Only Day of Salvation?* unpaged.
          "If You Die, Will You Live Again?" *The Plain Truth*,
          Mar. 1957, page 23.
          Lazarus and the Rich Man.

Chapter 6

Page 48   *The United States and the British Commonwealth in Prophecy,* Introduction, page xii.
49   *Ibid.,* page 164.
50   *Ibid.,* page 86
52   *Ibid.,* page 88.
57–58   *Ibid.,* pages 14–15.
59   *Ibid.,* pages 67–68.
63   *The Plain Truth,* July 1959, page 16.
64   *1975 in Prophecy,* pages 6–7, 10–12.
65   *Ibid.,* page 20.

Chapter 7

Page 67   *The Plain Truth,* Feb. 1960, page 26.
68   *Tomorrow's World,* Sept.–Oct. 1970, page 30.
  The Plain Truth, Feb. 1960, page 26.
68–69   *Why Marriage! . . . Soon Obsolete?* page 28.
71   *Tomorrow's World,* Sept.–Oct. 1970, page 31.

Chapter 8

Page 75   *Why Were You Born?* page 21.
76   *Ibid.,* pages 21, 22.
  Tomorrow's World, Sept.–Oct. 1970, page 31.
77   *Ibid.,* page 25.
  Ibid., page 28.
  Ibid., page 28.
78   *Why Marriage! . . . Soon Obsolete?* page 30.
78–79   *Ibid.,* pages 32–33.
83   *Ibid.*

Chapter 9

Page 85–86
  The Plain Truth About Christmas, page 12.
86   "Lent, Ashes, Easter, Rabbits, and Eggs—What's it all about?" *The Plain Truth,* April 1965, page 45.

73

87 *Why Marriage! . . . Soon Obsolete?* page 30.
88 "Why Celebrate Easter?" *The Plain Truth*, March 1966, page 30.
89 *Tomorrow's World*, March–April 1970, page 7. *If You Die, Will You Live Again?* page 2.

Chapter 10

Page 92 "What Is Worldliness?" *Tomorrow's World*, Sept. 1969, pages 22–23, 26–27.
93 *Ibid.*, pages 25–26.

Chapter 11

Page 101 Armstrong letters to his constituency, Sept. 26, 1969 and July 29, 1969.
103 *Which Day Is the Christian Sabbath?* page 58.

PB 247

DATE DUE